A field g
to
The English
Country Parson

Thomas Hinde

Phoebe Phillips/Heinemann

A Phoebe Phillips/Heinemann Book

First published in Great Britain in 1983
This edition published 1984

William Heinemann Ltd
10 Upper Grosvenor Street
London W1X 9PA
LONDON   MELBOURNE   TORONTO
JOHANNESBURG   AUCKLAND

434 98213 X

Designed by Playne Design

Illustrated by Maggie Colwell and
Jacquie Govier

Printed and bound in Great Britain by
Biddles Ltd, Guildford and King's Lynn

Introduction

Taken as a whole, country parsons suggest some sociological experiment: give a reasonably educated middle-class Englishman a modest income, a house in the country, and job security for life, and see what he will do. He does remarkable things. He becomes a world authority on spiders; he invents a theory of history which makes the Druids a tribe of Phoenician pre-Christian Christians; he plants 5,000 rose-bushes in his garden and the surrounding countryside, runs his own foxhound pack, makes his rectory into a monastery and turns Roman Catholic, collects folk-songs, breeds winning race-horses or green mice, rides from Land's End to John o' Groats . . . There seems no limit to the variety of his interests or to the obsessiveness with which he pursues them.

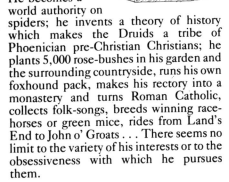

In recent times the country parson's power and influence have declined. Long ago he lost the support of the ecclesiastical courts when they ceased to be able to give wrong-doers meaningful sentences, and lost also the power to control his parishioners' behaviour which the confessional once gave him. Inflation has reduced the value of his income. Broadcasting, easy travel and secondary education have brought him parishioners with the confidence that they know at least as much as he does about the nature of the world and how to behave in it.

And yet he endures remarkably. Though many of his parishioners only visit his church three times in their lives – baptism, marriage and burial – he remains a symbol of community life. He also retains his ability to behave with a fine contempt for convention. In this century the Rev. Harold Davidson of Stiffkey was the grandest eccentric of all, and he has by no means been alone.

A high proportion of the parsons here described were eighteenth- and nineteenth-century men of good family; it has been said that the most important thing the Anglican Church gave England was a gentleman in every parish. Even today the country parson is often in this tradition. As a result it can easily be forgotten that for many centuries the village priest was hard to distinguish from the peasants around him.

In Saxon times, when the English parish system developed in the form of "ministers" established in the countryside by monasteries, the parson worked his strips of land like others in the village, with only the additional support of such offerings as "church scot" (paid by each householder after harvest), "soul scot" (paid at each death) and voluntary tithes. Until 1074 he was as free to marry as his parishioners.

His social status was to decline still further. Other parishes were founded by landowners on their estates, and after the Norman Conquest many such landowners, often with worthy intentions, gave these livings to the revitalized Cistercian and Cluniac monasteries of the times. In theory the monks were better able to supply priests and to supervise their work, but in practice the opposite happened: the monasteries took for themselves the rights of a living and employed a *vicarius* to work in the parish, paying him a starvation wage. It was not till 1215 that such "vicars" acquired security of tenure and received certain tithes, so beginning the process by which a vicar's position and that of a rector became more and more alike.

Throughout the Middle Ages it remained a regular complaint that the poor parson was ignorant, refused to wear clerical dress or be tonsured, and laboured on the land just like his parishioners. Apart from poverty, he had other problems. He competed with dubious sellers of pardons and relics, and with wandering friars who were often better educated. Nevertheless, as religious leader the parson held a position of some influence in the village. Sometimes he became the leader of revolt against monks, nobility and the Crown. And parish records show that many stayed to help their parishioners during the Black Death.

By the sixteenth century there had been little improvement in the education of country parsons, and the values of their livings had been reduced by inflation. They were also in short supply. Priests would often hold two or more livings, and employ curates to carry out their duties in the parishes where they did not reside.

Such curates were not the assistants to a vicar or rector who became common in the nineteenth century, but managed their parishes independently and were much like other country parsons except for their greater poverty and ignorance.

During the sixteenth century the country parson also faced the acute political and moral problems brought to him by the Reformation. Simon Aleyn, vicar of Bray, is typical of those who changed sides with

the times, as the English Church broke with Rome under Henry VIII, returned to Rome under Mary, then finally separated itself under Elizabeth. Others, less lucky or more principled, died as martyrs for their faith. Those who had taken the opportunity to marry when the Church allowed it in 1549, found the right repealed by Mary and were removed from their livings unless they put away their wives and did penance. Marriage for the clergy returned in Elizabethan times, but did not become legal till 1604.

By this time, the first half of the seventeenth century, the split between the Puritans (who favoured prayer, preaching, Bible-reading, purity of life and the observation of Sundays) and the High Church party (who favoured church ritual, believed in the supernatural quality of the sacrament of Holy Communion and preferred the celebration of saints' days) had become acute. William Laud, Archbishop of Canterbury from 1633 to 1641, led the High Church party, and there were many Laudian country parsons. The split was a principal cause of the Civil War, during which Laud was executed.

Wherever the Puritans were victorious they appointed committees to eject scandalous ministers, by which they meant any with Royalist or High Church sympathies. In total 2,425 clergy were ejected from their livings, many with great cruelty. Returning these parsons to their livings, and removing those who had taken their places, presented a problem at the Restoration. It was solved, not very satisfactorily, by the 1662 Act of Uniformity, the Bartholomew Act, which allowed those to stay who would publicly assent to the Book of Common Prayer. The 1,760 who refused came to form a solid body of Nonconformist Christians which existed from then onwards in rivalry to the established Church.

Those who remained Anglicans had fresh political problems during the rest of the century, particularly under James II, who again edged the Church towards Rome. The career of Francis Carswell, another

vicar of Bray and the one celebrated in the well-known song, suggests that some again chose to profess sympathy with whichever party in Church or state held power at the moment.

During Queen Anne's reign the country parson's social standing was uncertain. Only in Hanoverian times did he slowly but firmly become established as a gentleman, joint ruler of the village with the squire, one or other of them probably the local magistrate. The younger sons of good families began to go into the Church. Other parsons, even if they had no private money, found their parish dues and the profits from their glebe land more valuable than before and sufficient to give most of them a comfortable life. When the Napoleonic Wars (1805-1815) further drove up the price of agricultural produce, many became prosperous, and remained so until the agricultural depression of the 1880s.

Despite such new ease and prosperity, country parsons faced fresh problems from the middle of the eighteenth century when the Evangelicals, successors of the Puritans, again split the Church into High and Low factions. Like the Puritans, the Evangelicals distrusted the authority of the Church and its priests, and believed in a direct relationship between the individual and God. Many leading Evangelicals – Henry Venn, John Berridge, John Fletcher – held country livings. In their parishes, and up and down the country as visiting preachers, they expounded their doctrine of salvation by personal conversion, and produced by their inspired preaching amazing scenes of religious hysteria in their congregations. Some flirted with Methodism, or became Methodists.

The term Methodist originally described members of the "Holy Club" founded by the Wesley brothers at Oxford in 1729, but became used during the next 60 years to describe all who sympathised with the Wesleys and their movement. When, during the last ten years of the century, Methodism was fully established as a separate Church, it powerfully reinforced the old Nonconformists. Now some sort of Nonconformist Chapel, with its own congregation, became normal in most villages.

The Oxford Movement of the nineteenth century can be seen as a counter-attack by the High Church party. John Keble's 1833 sermon at St Mary's, Oxford, preached in front of the visiting judges of assize on Assize Sunday, is generally taken as its starting point. During the next eight years it circulated its views in publications known as *Tracts for the Times*. For this reason its sympathisers were called Tractarians. Though the Oxford Movement was university based, Keble himself was a country parson as were other keen Tractarians such as Thomas Mozley. Henry Manning was an Anglican country parson for many years, and although he, Newman and others found that their High Church views led them to Roman Catholicism, most Tractarians remained inside the Anglican Church. Their influence in reviving church ritual is proved by the Public Worship Regulations Act of 1874, which prohibited such Romish practices as the use of wafers instead of bread at Holy Communion, the setting of candles on the altar, the wearing by the clergy of ornate dress, and the taking of the "eastern position" during Holy Communion in which the priest stands to the west of the altar and faces east. The Act failed and the division of the clergy into High and Low has remained, even if today it rouses less passion.

Although many eighteenth- and nineteenth-century parsons prospered, others remained as poor as ever. In mediaeval times £10 a year (net) would have met a parson's living expenses, and this was his average income. However, he had other heavy liabilities: taxes to Rome and to the king, for example, and dues to his bishop as well as wages for his assistant curates. Regular efforts were made during the seventeenth century – before, during and after Cromwell's Commonwealth – to improve matters, but nothing effective was done till Queen Anne's reign. Then, in 1704, Queen Anne's Bounty was established.

Facts gathered for the governors of the Bounty give a clear idea of the situation at that time. Out of 9,180 livings, 1,216 were still worth less than £20, a further 2,610 worth less than £50 and and a further 1,256 less than £80 a year.

The governors obtained the right to certain Church revenues and were empowered to redistribute them, but for another century – till 1803 – they made this redistribution mainly by lottery rather than according to need. Forty years later, in 1844, the distributions were suspended for lack of funds, and not revived till the end of the century.

The result was that in the nineteenth century the incomes of country parsons continued to vary widely. At one end of the scale, Francis North held four livings worth a total of £3,140. At the other end, a poor curate like Thomas Teasdale of Luckington struggled to survive with five children on £80.

During the last century and a half the Church Commissioners have managed the Church's assets with considerable skill and have been able gradually to improve parsons' incomes. In 1908 they set a minimum for all benefices of £150 a year. Today, despite the loss of their tithes by the Tithe Redemption Act of 1936, incumbents earn a living wage, though not a generous one.

This, then, in simplified form, is the background against which most of the parsons in my selection pursued their calling. A proportion became involved in the dramatic events of their time. More developed their special interests and eccentricities in isolation, carrying out their Church functions in a routine way. Among those who took Holy Orders because it gave them financial security are George Crabbe, who was advised that he must find a way of life to support himself if he wished to be a poet, and Henry Manning, who would have preferred a political career but settled for the Church when his father's bankruptcy made that impossible. Many more – Sidney Smith, William Stukeley, Charles Kingsley (senior), for example – entered the Church with only the mildest sense of vocation.

With one exception I have stayed south of the Scottish border – Scottish ministers and the Church in Scotland are such a different story that they must be kept separate. On the other hand, I have strayed over the border into Wales – how could I leave out Francis Kilvert, R. S. Thomas or Daniel Rowlands?

I have avoided as many abstruse ecclesiastical terms as possible, but a few explanations may help readers unfamiliar with the Church of England and its history. Throughout I have used the word parson to describe any priest who ministered to a parish. Sometimes he was a rector – a mediaeval term which came to be used for a parson who had retained his rights to the parish tithes; sometimes a vicar who received for his keep an endowment, either in the form of money or certain tithes and part of the glebe land to farm; sometimes he might be a curate employed by an absentee parson to act for him. Or he might be a "perpetual curate", a priest who held a similar position to that of a vicar, but who had been appointed by a "lay rector". Lay rectors were patrons who had acquired the right to present priests to livings which had previously belonged to monasteries. A rector, vicar or perpetual curate is also called the incumbent of the living.

The living itself is often called a benefice. The right to present a priest to a particular benefice is known as an advowson. The person or institution which possesses this right of presentation is the patron of the living. The word "present" is used because the bishop may, for due cause, reject the patron's nomination. After the Reformation such rights of presentation might be held by a private individual, several individuals, a bishop, or the Crown. There was nothing to prevent a patron presenting himself to his own benefice.

Tithes were a form of tax consisting of a tenth of all agricultural produce. Their payment was made compulsory in England in 900. Great tithes were those on main crops like wheat and oats. Small tithes were on minor produce such as lambs and chickens. Parishioners paid them to the rector of the parish or, if the living had been appropriated to a monastery or impropriated to a lay rector, to the monastery or lay rector. The parson's glebe was

the land which went with the living, which he might farm himself or let to a tenant.

A country parson might, in addition to his living, spend part of his time working as a canon of a cathedral. Or he might become a prebendary, a position very like that of a canon, but in some cathedrals meaning a non-resident canon. Both appointments would bring him an additional salary. He might also be a rural dean and preside over meetings of parsons from neighbouring parishes. Such meetings were discussion groups and had no power. Or his bishop might appoint him as archdeacon, giving him authority over a particular territory, usually with a special responsibility for the fabric of its churches.

He might attend convocation, as a representative of the clergy of his diocese. The convocations of York and Canterbury were the Church of England's two assemblies. From the fifteenth century each sat as two houses, an upper house of bishops, and a lower one which included so-called proctors, each representing approximately a hundred clergy.

The ecclesiastical courts of the Church of England were described in 1883 as an unfathomable mystery. Certainly they defy brief summary; the Court of Arches, which I have sometimes mentioned, is the highest court of the province of Canterbury.

Finally, a word about the marrying duties of a parson. Until 1753 a marriage without any religious ceremony was valid, although outside the normal Church discipline. A highly profitable business in such secular marriages was carried out at Ludgate Hill and near the Fleet Prison, in London. Some parsons, with a surrogate power from their bishops, would marry couples without the usual banns, and make a handsome profit for themselves as well. The 1753 Act required all couples to have the banns called unless a special Bishop's licence was issued, but in Scotland this was not in force, and elopements continued north of the border until 1857, when the law there was changed to conform to English practice.

Civil and Nonconformist marriages were legalized in 1836, but even until the 1900s two-thirds of all marriages were solemnized by Anglican clergymen.

It only remains to apologise for omissions from my selection of country parsons. If the 10,000 parishes of England have had their individual incumbents for only half the past 500 years, and if a clergyman was on average beneficed for, say, forty years of his life, I have had some 60,000 from which to choose. The field has been embarrassingly rich and I can only hope that my sample, despite, or because of, its variety, is representative.

How to trace your local parson

Readers who want to discover more about their local parsons and parish history should look in their parish records, still sometimes kept by the parson but now more often housed by the diocese at the County Records Office. The records of bishops' visitations to their parishes, often more interesting, are usually kept here too. H.M.S.O.publishes a booklet, *Record Repositories in Great Britain*, which says where most records of this sort are housed.

In addition, readers can go to past editions of *Crockford's Clerical Directory*, first published in 1858, or to the *Clergy Lists*, first published in 1841. Here they can trace particular clergymen, or the incumbents of a particular parish at a particular time. In three previous years, 1817, 1829 and 1836, a *Clerical Guide and Ecclesiastical Directory* was published, and in 1808, 1809 and 1810 an *Ecclesiastical and Universities Annual Register*.

If a clergyman has been well enough known to appear in the *Dictionary of National Biography* the bibliography at the end of his entry may lead to further sources.

Where a church has been closed or a parish amalgamated with another, the latest edition of *Crockford* usually explains what has happened and who is now the priest in charge.

James Williams Adams
Postwick, Norfolk

James Adams (1839-1905) was the the first clergyman to be awarded the Victoria Cross. He won it during the Afghan War, for first rescuing a wounded lancer under heavy fire from among many wounded Afghans who slashed at him as he passed, and then, still under "an accurate and galling fire" rescuing two more lancers, both trapped below their horses and drowning. He was "as cool as a cucumber the whole day."

In India he worked gallantly in smallpox camps, attributing his escape from the disease to seven yearly inoculations and a glass of sherry each time he entered a camp. Once when burying smallpox and cholera victims he stepped backwards and disappeared into an open grave. Not a soldier present dared laugh. He also hunted, collecting his own scratch pack at Peshawar and using it to pursue jackal.

Postwick was the Norfolk parish he returned to, and he held the living there from 1887 to 1894. He was not a great preacher, being a man unskilled with words. In the pulpit he had a "curious and irritating cough" which he did not have at other times.

He next took on the livings of Wimbotsham and Stow Bardolph. When, after his death, Stow Mission Church was built, his wife gave to it the portable altar and credence tables which he had used in battle during the Afghan War. Here they are still preserved. Here, too, he is commemorated on a tablet erected by his old general and military colleague, Lord Roberts.

Simon Aleyn
Bray, Berkshire

"The Vicar of Bray will be Vicar of Bray still" was a Berkshire proverb from before the Civil War. It referred to Simon Aleyn, who had been the vicar there from 1540 to 1588, under Henry VIII, Edward VI, Mary and Elizabeth, and who was first a Papist, then a Protestant, then a Papist, and then a Protestant again. Thomas Fuller wrote that Aleyn "had seen some Martyrs burnt (two miles off) at Windsor, and found this fire too hot for his tender temper". When accused of being a turncoat, Aleyn replied: "Not so for I alwaies kept my principle, which is this, to live and die the Vicar of Bray."

Wilbert Vere Awdry
Emneth, Norfolk

W. V. Awdry (b. 1911) author of *Thomas the Tank Engine* and twenty-five other train books, began to invent these stories to tell his son of three who had measles. Presently he wrote them down to help him remember them and then was persuaded by his wife to send them to an agent. Eighteen months later the first four were accepted by a publisher and all are still in print.

At this time Awdry was a curate of King's Norton, Birmingham, but he had been interested in railways since he was four, when his father, also a country parson and railway enthusiast, would take him walking along the track at Baddesley Bridge near Ampfield. Later at Box he would lie

in bed at night listening to the engines talking to each other as they laboured up the one-in-a-hundred gradient on the Great Western's London to Bristol line which passed 200 yards away.

At Emneth, where he was vicar for twelve years from 1953, his parishioners mostly regarded him with "a kind of amused tolerance, as to someone a bit cracked but otherwise quite harmless". To encourage this view and enliven Parochial Church Council meetings he would report to them in doggerel verse, for example:

It's four years since our Vicar came,
And we have gone on much the same . . .
He's neither "High" nor very "Low",
Some people think he's rather slow;
They wonder if he's any brains
He's intr'sted in Railway Trains!
And he writes books about them too
We rather think he's lost a screw . . .

They were grateful, however, when he exhibited his model railway at fairs and fêtes and brought back money for parish appeals.

He fitted the writing of his annual railway book into the quiet time of the church year between the end of August and the first Sunday in Advent. When his child (and adult) readers began to find discrepancies between the illustrations of his stories and their real settings he invented the Island of Sodor, lying between Barrow-in-Furness and the Isle of Man, complete with its own railway system. The island has grown in reality and now has not only villages and towns but industry, geology, politics and an economy. Lately he has begun to give lectures on *Pages from Sodor History*. In retirement his house at Stroud is named Sodor and his notepaper carries a print of "Sydney and Parramatta Railway Loco No. 1."

Edward Bagshaw
Ambrosden, Oxfordshire

Edward Bagshaw (1629-71) began early to give evidence of his awkward nature when at Christ Church, Oxford he showed insolence towards the vice-chancellor and was prominent in an agitation for the abolition of hoods and caps. As second master of Westminster School he was involved in a great row with the headmaster, Dr Richard Busby, who accused him of wearing his hat in church, and taking "a strange delight in whipping". Bagshaw was dismissed by Dr Busby, who published his own version of the strange affair.

His brief period as vicar of Ambrosden ended in 1662 when he elected to be one of those ejected by the Bartholomew Act. The same year he was arrested and confined to the Tower for abusing the King, government, church and state. When released he was promised considerable preferment in the Church if he would live quietly in the country for a year, but this was more than he could manage and he was soon back in prison, this time Newgate, for refusing to take the Oath of Supremacy and Allegiance to the King.

Bagshaw married a blind gentlewoman who had fallen in love with his preaching, but he was still on parole from prison when he died in Tothill Street, Westminster. He was buried in Bunhill Fields; the inscription for his tomb concluded: "From the reproaches of pretended friends, and persecutions of professed adversaries, he took sanctuary, by the will of God, in eternal rest."

Charles F. Bampfylde
Dunkerton, Cornwall

Charles Bampfylde, rector of Dunkerton from 1820 to 1855, was known as "The Devil of Dunkerton". John Skinner, his fellow parson, believed there was not a more worthless fellow in the West of England. He was, Skinner wrote, the bastard of a worthless, unprincipled man, and had openly participated in the libertinism of his father. It was scandalous that, because of "undue influence", such a man should be provided for in the Church.

Richard Harris Barham
Snargate, Kent

This agreeable but indolent man (1788-1845), remembered as the author of *The Ingoldsby Legends*, came to the living of Snargate in the Romney Marsh in 1817. Here two years later he wrote a novel, *Baldwin*, to relieve boredom after an accident had confined him to his house. The book was soon forgotten. Fifteen years later he finished a second novel, *My Cousin Nicholas*, only because a friend had begun without his permission to serialize its early chapters.

Similarly, he started to write *The Ingoldsby Legends* to provide stories and poems for a school friend and publisher, Bentley. When he heard that Bentley's magazine, which was to have been called *The Wits' Miscellany* was in fact to be called *Bentley's Miscellany*, Barham asked, "Why go to the other extreme?"

Many of the humorous and fantastic tales and verses which make up *The Ingoldsby Legends* – of which *The Jackdaw of Rheims* is the best known – drew on Barham's knowledge of his native Kent. His parish was notorious for smuggling and at one time a large amount of tobacco was found in the church belfry, and a keg of hollands under the vestry table. The *Legends* were accompanied by the drawings of such illustrious illustrators of Dickens as Cruikshank and Leech. A first series was collected in 1840, and two further series in 1847, but by then Barham had died of a cold caught at the opening of the Royal Exchange.

Sabine Baring-Gould
Lew Trenchard, Devon

Sabine Baring-Gould (1834-1924) was a man of phenomenal energy. Driven on by an enormous family, extravagance, generosity, and financial incompetence, he had by his mid-eighties published 159 books. He was antiquarian, architect, early pot-holer, hymn writer, folk song collector and land-owning squire. In 1881 he presented himself to his own benefice of Lew Trenchard, went to live in his own manor known as Lew House and stayed there for the rest of his life, dying at the age of ninety.

Until he was seventeen he had no home but continuously toured the Continent with his parents, learning many languages but getting little formal education. At Cambridge he became a Tractarian but his plan to take Holy Orders was opposed by his father who believed that a first son should manage the family estates. Cut off from family support, he became a schoolmaster, first in Pimlico, later at Hurstpierpoint in Sussex.

Baring-Gould's first curacy was at Horbury Brig in Yorkshire where the population consisted largely of canal boatmen, colliers and mill workers. Here he wrote *Onward, Christian Soldiers*, first sung by the children of the parish at a Whitsun procession, and further alienated his father by marrying an eighteen-year-old clog-wearing mill-girl sixteen years younger than himself.

For ten years from 1871 he held the Crown living of East Mersea in Essex, given to him by Gladstone, who thought well of his controversial book *The Origin and Development of Religious Belief*. He set his best novel, *Medalah*, a tale of hatred, violence and passion, in the Essex salt marshes. At East Mersea he also wrote a sixteen-volume hagiography containing the biographies of 3,600 saints; he received £50 a volume, and this not paid regularly, since his publisher went bankrupt during publication.

He continued to write at Lew Trenchard, always standing to do this at a specially constructed desk in his library. Apart from forty novels, he published guide books, biographies, books on caves, religious works and *Songs of the West*, a volume of folk songs, some of them improved or bowdlerized, which he had collected from over sixty ancient Devon and Cornish song-men. His book on the Roman emperors is less easily categorized. Purporting to be historical biography, it was a work of imagination, based on inspirations derived from looking at busts of the emperors and running his hands over their craniums, hence deducing their characters and likely actions.

Baring-Gould has been accused by some (including Sir John Betjeman) of stealing the Gould family memorials from Staverton church to set them up in his own, but others say he saved them from destruction. Certainly he rebuilt Lew Trenchard

church, as well as many of his farms and farm cottages, designing these himself and forgetting to put front doors in two of them. He was so reduced financially by such extravagances that in 1901 he was forced to sell his horses, shut his house and live for a time in France.

In all he had fifteen children, the oldest daughter being married in the same year that the youngest was born. When young men came courting his daughters he would discomfort them with amusing tricks, for example a device consisting of two inflatable rubber bladders connected by a tube. One of these he would lay flat below the tablecloth in the guest's place, the other hold himself below the table. This he would secretly compress, so setting the young man's soup mysteriously rocking.

Lew House is still in his family. At one time a hotel, it is now open to the public as a historic manor.

William Barnes
Winterborne Came, Dorset

The poet, William Barnes (1801-86), son of a tenant farmer in the Vale of Blackmore, showed such intellectual promise that he was able to obtain work in a solicitor's office in Dorchester. Here he began to publish verses in the local *Weekly Entertainer* and learned to make woodcuts. Presently he became a schoolmaster. He was a prodigious linguist and taught himself Anglo-Saxon, Welsh, French, Italian, Persian, Russian, Hebrew and Hindustani. The Dorset dialect became his special interest. He wrote a number of vernacular poems and translated *The Song of Solomon* into Dorset.

He was a linguistic purist, opposed to Latin and Greek derivatives. For "bicycle" and "photograph" he would have preferred "wheelsaddle" and "sunprint".

Barnes only took Holy Orders in 1847 and obtained his Cambridge divinity degree in 1850. Eleven years later he was given the Dorset living of Winterborne Came, where he remained for the rest of his life. On market days in Dorchester he was a familiar figure, walking usually in the middle of the street in caped coat, knee-breeches and buckled shoes, with leather satchel, stout staff and a little grey dog at his heels. He was buried in Came churchyard and a statue was erected to him in the churchyard of St Peter's, Dorchester. Coventry Patmore wrote of him, "He has done a small thing well, while his contemporaries have mostly been engaged in doing big things ill."

John Berridge
Everton, Bedfordshire

John Berridge (1716-93) was the son of a Nottinghamshire grazier, but his father despaired of teaching him this trade and sent him instead to Clare Hall, Cambridge. Here he took Holy Orders and presently obtained the living of Everton. After two years at Everton he abandoned written sermons and began to preach salvation by "faith" rather than "works". The effects were sensational: "Some of his hearers cried out aloud hysterically, some were thrown into strong convulsions, and some fell into a kind of trance or catalepsy, which lasted a long time."

Thereafter he preached throughout East Anglia, often in the open, to audiences of thousands, becoming a leading Evangelical in the manner of the Wesley brothers, Daniel Rowlands and other Methodists. Like them, he angered the parsons in whose parishes he preached, but when the bishop of his diocese threatened to dispossess him, he was protected by the elder Pitt, whose friend he had been at Cambridge.

Unlike some Methodists, he resisted marriage, and wrote that there was "no trap so mischievous to the field-preacher as wedlock; and it is laid for him at every hedge corner. Matrimony has quite maimed poor Charles [Wesley], and might have spoiled John [Wesley] and George [Whitefield], if a wise Master had not graciously sent them a brace of ferrets . . . Eight or nine years ago, having been grievously tormented with house-keeping, I truly thought of looking out for a Jezebel myself. But it seemed needful to ask advice of the Lord."

He found the Lord's advice in Jeremiah XVI:2:"Thou shalt not take thee a wife, neither shalt thou have sons or daughters in this place."

Berridge died at the age of seventy-seven and was buried at his own request on the north-east side of Everton churchyard, as "a means of consecrating it". This piece of ground had previously been reserved for those who had come to a dishonourable end.

John Birkbie
Moor Monkton, Yorkshire

John Birkbie, rector of Moor Monkton in the mid-sixteenth century, was one of those Tudor parsons who aroused anger by their ornate style of dressing. Despite the Royal Injunction of 1559, which ordered clergy to wear cassock, gown, tippet and square cap, he would appear in "very undecent apparell namelie great britches cut and drawne oute with sarcenet and taffite and great ruffes laid on with laceis of gold and silk." Furthermore he was said to be a fornicator and a drunkard, and to be in the habit of dancing offensively in alehouses.

Francis Blomefield
Fersfield, Norfolk

Francis Blomefield (1705-52), historian of Norfolk and rector of Fersfield from 1729 till his death, printed his *History of Norfolk* on his own press at Fersfield rectory. "I don't care one farthing", he wrote, "if I print my work in a manner to my own liking . . . I don't print (I thank God for it) for my bread, having a comfortable subsistence independent of all men."

Nevertheless Blomefield got into financial difficulties, partly because he was also a hunting man and kept his own pack of hounds. When he died at the age of forty-seven, half way through writing the third volume of his history, he was so much in debt that his executors would not act but handed over the administration of his estate to his two chief creditors. He died from smallpox, caught on a visit to London for research; he had refused to be inoculated and thus avoid an evil sent by God. He lies buried in the chancel of Fersfield church.

Nicholas Bownde
Norton, Suffolk

Nicholas Bownde (d. 1613), rector of Norton from 1585 for twenty-five years, published his stern views on Sunday behaviour in *The True Doctrine of the Sabbath*. On the seventh day Christians were as bound to rest as Jews are. There should be no "interludes, May-games, morris dancing, shooting, bowling or similar sport" and no feasting, except by "noblemen and great personages". The Sabbatarian question was the first point of doctrine on which the High Church party differed from the Puritans. In 1611 Bownde moved to St Andrew the Apostle, Norwich where he died and was buried.

William Bridges
Gotham, Nottinghamshire

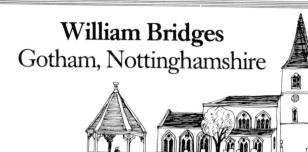

In 1743 William Bridges (1678-1746), rector of Gotham, wrote to Archbishop Herring of York to complain of the size of his rectory "which indeed is a very great one, as yr Grace may be pleas'd to observe . . . the greatest I believe in your Diocese . . . I have six score windows in the dwelling House, 8 Stairs Cases, and not one good one; an hundred Doors made out of Sawn Boards, on ye Premisses." He had succeeded his father as rector in 1710. The archbishop also records that he had "two very good women but sickly wives". He, his parents and his wives are commemorated by a tablet in Gotham church.

Patrick Brontë
Haworth, Yorkshire

Patrick Brontë (1777-1861), father of Charlotte, Emily and Anne, was born in a remote part of County Down, to which his own father, a Protestant, had eloped with his mother, a Catholic. He was the eldest of their ten children.

As tutor to the children of the rector of Drumgooland he saved up £25 and then sent himself to St John's College, Cambridge, where he took Holy Orders. After holding a number of curacies, at the age of forty-three he obtained the living of the remote Yorkshire parish of Haworth.

Here he was a stern father to his six children, feeding them on potatoes without meat to make them hardy. On one occasion he burned their boots because he considered them too smart; also a silk gown of his wife's. Suffering from indigestion, he commonly dined alone. To relieve his feelings he would sometimes smash up pieces of furniture. He slept always with a loaded pistol by his bed, a habit acquired during the Luddite troubles of 1812. At dawn he would discharge this from his bedroom window towards the church tower (his bullets' marks can still be seen) to the surprise of his parishioners.

Brontë's family life was tragic. His wife died of cancer the year after he came to Haworth. His two elder daughters died at the ages of ten and eleven of consumption contracted at a nearby school for the children of the clergy. Twenty-three years later his son Branwell, and Emily and Anne all died of consumption within eight months of each other. Charlotte survived longest, dying in 1855. It was once assumed that she also died of consumption but today morning-sickness is thought the more probable cause. She had married A.B. Nicholls, Brontë's curate, just nine months before, a marriage which Brontë had previously forbidden, only allowing it when compelled by her pining. He survived all his children by six years, a lonely old man, but sustained by the increasing reputation of his daughters' works.

Joseph Heathcote Brooks
Great Rollright, Oxfordshire

Joseph Brooks (1812-1855), appointed rector of Great Rollright in 1848, was one of those Victorian clergymen who believed that his parsonage should represent better his place in society. In 1849 he pulled down the seventeenth-century rectory and began to build a more ambitious one. It was to have a large airy living room, a wide staircase and enormous cellars. These astonished visitors and were more like the crypt of a church than the cellars of a private house. While supervising the building he would encourage his workmen with such cries as "Give me air-give me space! Enlarge it here! Enlarge it there!"

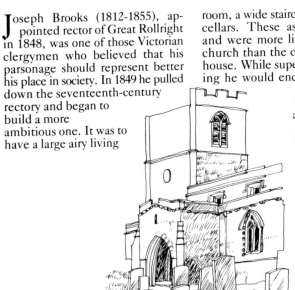

As a result he became heavily in debt. For fear of local creditors he would only leave his rectory on Sundays, and then only to cross to the church by way of the vegetable garden. At Matins one Sunday in 1851 he began his sermon with the text, "Forgive us our debts as we forgive our debtors", disappeared into the vestry and was seen no more. He left the country and died from an accident four years later in Prussia, where he fell through the trapdoor of an upper room and was killed "upon the spot".

Brooks' rectory stood until the 1960s when it was largely pulled down by Charlie Jeffries, a well-known local poacher, though a small part is still incorporated in the house now called The Old Rectory.

Francis Rosslyn Courtenay Bruce
Herstmonceux, Sussex

Rosslyn Bruce (1871-1956), rector of Herstmonceux for thirty-three years from 1923 till he died at eighty-five, was obsessed all his life with animals. When a curate at St Anne's, Soho, his first sermon was advertised as *Do Animals Live After Death?* He argued that they must, since they were an essential part of himself, and if they did not, only part of him could go to heaven.

At Oxford, when told by the junior proctor that dogs were forbidden in college, Bruce rented a cow and walked it round the quad. Rona, a Skye terrier, who in spite of the rule had puppies under his college bed, won her terrier class at Crufts the same week that he was elected Secretary of the Oxford Union. He also kept a young elephant in a shed for scientific purposes. It was just like keeping a rabbit, he said, except that it had "a hundred rabbit power eating capacity". He helped pay for its keep by getting stale buns from a baker and selling them to visitors to feed to it.

In London where he was first a curate, Bruce frequently preached from theatre stages, and one music hall even allowed him four minutes.

When he arrived at Clifton he at once acquired a horse, a gun dog and several cages of ferrets. He befriended the Nottinghamshire miners and took a keen interest in "The Fancy", their homing pigeon clubs. He would carry birds and beasts in his pockets and occasionally loose a dove from his surplice when preaching to illustrate "the flight of love".

He left his menagerie at Clifton to take a living at Edgbaston, near Birmingham, but acquired more animals during his eleven years there. When he moved again to Herstmonceux many of these came with him in his new Ford. A goat gave birth to two kids on the way.

At Herstmonceux his animals, especially the dogs, proliferated. He wrote books about them, including his classic *Fox Terrier Breeding, the Line and Family Method*, in which he argued that "the dam's dam's dam is the chief factor in a pedigree over and above the sire's sire's sire". He contributed a weekly nature column to *The Evening Standard* and wrote a hunting column for the local paper signed "Old Dog Fox". He changed the name of the village Sunday School to the Ministering Children's League. On its annual picnics at Pevensey Bay the members would bury their rector in the sand, taking care not to cover his nose.

Late in life Bruce completed a long breeding experiment by producing a green mouse. This so interested the press that he persuaded one credulous reporter that he had also crossed a bat successfully with a mouse, which would soon give birth to a "bouse".

One of his sisters, Kathleen, married Captain Scott, the antarctic explorer, making Sir Peter Scott, painter and naturalist, his nephew. He had five children of his own and named his eldest daughter Rhalou. He invented the name, he would say, from his war-time army unit, the Royal Horse Artillery Liverpool Ordnance Unit. In fact Rhalou was born before the war and named after Bruce's grandmother, a Greek princess.

When he was dying in hospital his daughter, Verily Anderson, brought him an early copy of her first book. He could write a better one than that, he said, but he was more gracious about a mouse she had brought to play on his bed; the light through its beautiful little ears was like the gates of heaven.

Evelyn Henry Villebois Burnaby
Burrough on the Hill, Leicestershire

In 1892 Evelyn Burnaby, vicar of Burrough on the Hill in Quorn country from 1873 to 1883, rode from Land's End to John o'Groats. Weighing sixteen stone, he played out three horses in the process. The Royal Society for the Prevention of Cruelty to Animals protested, but did not prevent him from finishing. Burnaby's real interest was the law and he went reluctantly into the Church, in order to take up the family living at Burrough. But for fifty years he regularly attended all the most sensational murder cases of the time. Court officials regularly reserved a special seat for him. As well as an account of his ride, he published *Memories of Famous Trials*.

Charles Butler
Wootton St Lawrence, Hampshire

Charles Butler (*c.* 1560-1647), vicar of Wootton St Lawrence for forty-seven years, published in 1609 his successful book on bees, *The Feminine Monarchy*. In it he described his discovery that worker bees were female and drones male. He believed that the queen ruled the hive but did not understand that she was its mother. He advised bee keepers "Thou must not come among them smelling of sweat, or having a stinking breath, caused either through eating leeks, onions or garlic". The book was so successful that he was able to give his daughter, whom he called his "sweet honey girl", a dowry of £400. This daughter was the great-grandmother of the Rev Gilbert White, naturalist of Selborne. Butler had previously attempted but failed to make money by keeping silk worms. At this time he lived in a "poor Vicarage, God Wot, for so worthy a scholar".

Butler's scholarship included music – he published *The Principles of Music* – and grammar; his *English Grammar* was admired by Dr Johnson. Although a Laudian, he was permitted to retain his living by the Parliamentarians.

Francis Carswell
Bray, Berkshire

Simon Aleyn was the sixteenth-century vicar of Bray whose religious fluctuations gave the saying its popular meaning, but the well-known song (written in about 1720 by an officer in Colonel Fuller's regiment) describes Dr Francis Carswell, vicar of Bray more than a hundred years later, from 1667 to 1709.

In the song the vicar claims to have been a High Churchman under Charles II, a Papist under James II, a Protestant again under William, a Tory under Anne and a Whig under George I. The last suggestion must, however, have been invention, since Carswell had ceased to hold the living by the date of George's accession.

Edmund Cartwright
Goadby Marwood, Leicestershire

Edmund Cartwright (1743-1823), a resourceful inventor, who among other things built a power-loom without ever having seen a hand-loom, was for many years poorly rewarded for his ingenuity.

At Oxford he made a reputation as a poet and volumes of his poems were later published. In 1779 he obtained the living of Goadby Marwood, which he held for twenty-nine years. His career as an inventor began on a visit to Arkwright's spinning mill at Matlock in Derbyshire where he remarked to Arkwright that it would be as easy to make a weaving machine as it had been "to construct the automatic chess player". Presumably he referred to von Kempelen's The Automaton Chess Player (The Turk) which first appeared at the Austrian Court in 1780.

In 1785, he took out a patent for his own power-loom, a clumsy but effective machine; two years later, having failed to interest manufacturers in it, he set up a factory in Doncaster, a town he chose because his wife owned property there. Here he installed an improved model which, though not the first power-loom as is sometimes said, was the earliest to weave wide cloth like calico for practical purposes.

Cartwright next invented a wool-combing machine which did the work of twenty men; it so threatened the jobs of the wool-combers that 50,000 petitions against it were received by the House of Commons. At this time a manufacturer who had ordered 400 of Cartwright's power-looms had his factory in Manchester burned down, probably by intention. As a result of such opposition Cartwright became deeply in debt and had to dispose of his Doncaster mill.

Though he then invented a reaping machine and was encouraged in other agricultural experiments by the Duke of Bedford at Woburn, he remained poor until, in 1809, Parliament belatedly voted him a reward of £10,000. He is buried in the church at Battle, Sussex.

William Cole
Bletchley, Buckinghamshire

William Cole (1714-82), antiquary, friend of Horace Walpole and Roman Catholic sympathizer, would have liked to live in Normandy, but was dissuaded by the fact that the French king would have acquired rights to his collection of manuscripts. Instead, in 1853 he took the living of Bletchley. Though he considered that this cost him "fifteen years of the best part of my life", he was a responsible parson especially concerned about his parishioners' health.

Ultimately Cole left a hundred folio volumes to the British Museum. In compiling these he wrote that he was "wearing my eyes, fingers and self out in writing for posterity". They mainly concern the history of Cambridgeshire where he had subsequently gone to live, but they were also sprinkled with such vitriolic comments on his friends and acquaintances that he required the volumes to remain unseen until twenty years after his death. Of Bishop Green of Lincoln he wrote: "This squeamish Bp after giving his Nephew a good Sine-cure Hospital at Northampton, and this living of Stoke-Goldington with Gayhurst annexed, within six weeks . . . gave him another equally good Living in Northamptonshire called Wappenham. This loading with Preferments, all of a sudden, a young Man, of no Behaviour or Appearance, gave no small scandal at our Visitation in June; where the Nephew exhibited his extraordinary Self for the first Time."

Richard Conyers
Helmsley, Yorkshire

Richard Conyers, eighteenth-century rector of the large parish of Helmsley, saw "the light" on Christmas Day 1758, when he became so excited that he ran about his parsonage calling out "I have found Him, I have found Him". His subsequent innovations in the parish included the periodic ringing of the church bell, at the sound of which farm labourers were to stop their work and pray. The Archbishop of York was less than enthusiastic about Conyers' conversion and on hearing him preach told him that such stuff would drive his parish-

Hugh Palisser Costobadie
King's Norton, Leicestershire

In 1839 Hugh Costobadie (1804-87), known to his friends as the "Reverend Costo", set a record. In a single day he rode forty miles, jumped four gates, took four services and shot two wild ducks. He arrived home after dark with the ducks hanging from his saddle.

He moved from Hallaton where he created his record, first to be British chaplain at Koblenz, and then to King's Norton where he held the living from 1844 for forty-three years. Here a windfall suddenly put an end to his financial troubles and he went about Leicester with his hat full of pound notes, paying off his debts to the baker, butcher and other tradesmen.

George Crabbe
Muston, Leicestershire

Though George Crabbe (1754-1832) held the living of Muston for twenty-five years, and later that of Trowbridge for the last eighteen years of his life, he is more often associated with the small Suffolk fishing town of Aldeburgh which was the subject of his best known poems, and where he was born, the son of the collector of salt taxes. Here as a young man he was apprenticed to two neighbouring doctors and also worked in the warehouses on the quays. After a visit to London to "pick up a little surgical knowledge" he set up his own medical practice in Aldeburgh.

Growing impatient with this, he again sailed on a lugger to London to try to live by writing, taking with him £3 in cash, a box of surgical instruments and a few manuscript poems. Here he became increasingly poor and was forced to sell his instruments and books. He appealed for help to leading politicians of the time, including Lord North, but all refused him. Eventually he wrote to Burke saying that he was about to be sent to prison for a debt of £14. Burke rescued him, helped him to publish his poems, had him to stay at Beaconsfield, his country home, and advised him to take Holy Orders. In 1782 he was ordained and returned to Aldeburgh as curate.

He was not happy here, where he was remembered too well as the doctor who had drunk merrily with soldiers of the local military garrison, so he moved to the Vale of Belvoir, where the Duke of Rutland offered him first a chaplaincy and then the living of Muston. He took the living with relief since as chaplain at Belvoir Castle he had been "snubbed both by servants and guests". Here

he was happiest, and his son George, who wrote his biography, remembered him "absorbed in the arrangement of his minerals, shells and insects; especially 'fungi' and 'petrifications'". Meanwhile he had published *The Village*, a poem of realism ahead of its time, which made him some reputation.

For twelve out of his twenty-five years at Muston he was an absentee, returning to live again near Aldeburgh. Eventually he came back to Muston when the pressure on non-resident clergy increased. During all this time he wrote continuously, but for twenty-two years published nothing, holding instead periodic "incremations", a habit "less common than might be wished". His children, the two out of the seven who lived, helped him with these burnings of manuscripts "too vast to be safely consumed in the chimney". In this way an essay on botany and three partly finished novels were lost. In 1809, however, he published *The Parish Register* and next year *The Borough*. His shorter poems include *Sir Eustace Grey*, inspired by an opium dream. He had been taking opium since it was prescribed after a collapse in the street at Ipswich.

In 1814 the Duke of Rutland persuaded Crabbe to exchange Muston for Trowbridge in Wiltshire. By this time Crabbe's wife had died and he spent much emotional energy in trying to find another. For a time he was engaged to Charlotte Ridout, thirty-five years his junior. "I have", he wrote, ". . . six female friends unknown to each other, but all dear, very dear to me." His biographer suggests twelve possible candidates, but he died a widower. He is buried in the churchyard at Trowbridge.

William Barker Daniel

If W.B. Daniel (1753-1833) was ever beneficed his living has not been discovered, but his extensive interest and knowledge of country matters is proved by his book *Rural Sports*. This, first published in 1801, delighted sportsmen at the beginning of the nineteenth century; it covered all matters relating to sport from dogs, foxes, deer and hares to game birds and contained much strange information. It describes, for example, the custom in the north of England of tying up a bitch in season where a dog fox could serve her. The hybrids which resulted were "much esteemed for their handiness in driving cattle; they bite keenly, are extremely active and playful, and are very expert at destroying Weazels, Rats and other Vermin."

In 1813 Daniel published a supplementary volume, nominally on fishing but containing even more anecdotal matter. In Morayshire, he writes, a young girl called "Red Jean" determined to become a man and began to shave. In tartan philabeg, short coat and blue bonnet "she exhibited the Apperance of a flashy *young man*". When mocked by the young of the neighbourhood she retaliated with corporal punishment, "she being no mean *Proficient* in the heroic art of Pugilism".

Even in his own tolerant times Daniel's exclusive interest in sporting as opposed to spiritual matters raised adverse comment. Recognizing this perhaps, he published in 1822 *Plain Thoughts of Former Years upon the Lord's Prayer*.

George Dauglish
Standlake, Oxfordshire

During the Second World War George Dauglish (1904-76), rector of Standlake from 1936 to 1947, became embroiled in a prolonged quarrel with Sir Henry Chitty, occupant of The Manor. "That man makes me see red", Sir Henry wrote, confirming that personal dislike lay below the specific causes of their disagreement. Dauglish was plump, with a large scar across one side of his pale round face. He was unmarried and lived with his old mother in the large rectory beside the river Windrush.

The quarrel began one Harvest Festival when, according to Sir Henry's wife, Ethel, "after reminding us of his sermons for the past three Sundays and giving us a summary of the weather for the year, he spent the rest of his sermon rating the children for their bad behaviour and reading long extracts from *Martin Chuzzlewit*. We were told the children were rude, bad-mannered, destructive, disrespectful – and that 'small boys brought out their Damns and their bloodies' quite regardless of whether he [George] was listening or not – it was a dreadful very un-Christian performance."

Soon, however, the quarrel centred around Dauglish's insistence that Confirmation candidates should attend church *every* Sunday, and repeat the Catechism to him after the second lesson. This provided Sir Henry with an excuse to start a rival children's service on Sunday evenings in the village hall. His service was broadly based, allowing Nonconformists to attend, and consisted largely of hymn singing. At first nominally for children, it was soon patronized by adults too. Congregations grew from seventy-three at the start to 200 during one "War Weapons Week", when the village "marched to our service, not to George's church".

In spite of this success, Sir Henry continued to consult the rural dean and the Bishop of Dorchester in the hope of having Dauglish replaced, and to complain that there was no way to remove a Church of England parson unless he was drunk in the pulpit. He was right. Dauglish was still rector of Standlake when Sir Henry left the village for a mental hospital.

Harold Davidson
Stiffkey, Norfolk

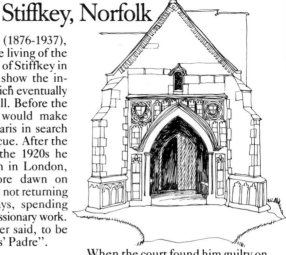

Harold Davidson (1876-1937), who obtained the living of the remote Norfolk parish of Stiffkey in 1906, began early to show the interest in fallen girls which eventually led to his own downfall. Before the First World War he would make fortnightly visits to Paris in search of suitable girls to rescue. After the war and throughout the 1920s he continued his mission in London, travelling there before dawn on Monday mornings and not returning until late on Saturdays, spending night and day at his missionary work. He was proud, he later said, to be called the "Prostitutes' Padre".

Others thought less well of him; investigators were hired to follow him and one of them, after feeding a certain Rose Ellis eight glasses of port, extracted a scandalous story from her. Davidson wrote letters in his own defence, Rose Ellis withdrew her accusation, but not in time to prevent Davidson publishing his full story in the *Empire News*. By now the press were accusing him of immoral practices with over a thousand girls. His fame grew, his church congregation at Stiffkey swelled to 500, and in February 1932 one coachload travelled from as far as Bournemouth to hear him preach.

Davidson was brought before the Consistory Court, sitting in the Great Hall of Church House, Westminster. Here his trial lasted over four months and was reported at length each day in the press. In June when the chancellor retired to consider his summing up, Davidson returned to Stiffkey and ejected a clergyman sent to minister in his absence. Later that month he was granted permission to give recitations to audiences of up to two thousand at Birmingham.

When the court found him guilty on all five charges he went to Blackpool and sat in a barrel for fourteen hours a day to raise money for his appeal. He was fined for obstruction. Returning once more to Stiffkey, he was kicked down the front steps by his churchwarden, Major Hammond. The Major was fined twenty shillings for assault.

On the day of his ceremonial defrocking at Norwich Cathedral, Davidson sent a telegram to say he would be late, then when he arrived, he continuously interrupted the bishop during the proceedings. In the procession to the high altar he forced his way forward and supplanted the bishop.

Three years later in the summer of 1935 Davidson and his daughter Pamela returned to Blackpool to enter adjoining fasting cages. They were arrested and charged with attempted suicide, but the charge failed and Davidson was awarded £382 damages against Blackpool Corporation. At Skegness Amusement Park in the summer of 1937, when speaking to the public from inside a lion's cage, the lion, whose name was Freddie, attacked him and severely injured his head and neck. Freddie's keeper, sixteen-year-old Irene, rescued Davidson but he died two days later in Skegness Cottage Hospital.

John Dee
Upton upon Severn, Worcestershire

John Dee (1527-1608) may never have taken Holy Orders, but he held the livings of Upton upon Severn and Long Leadenham for many years. During Queen Mary's reign he was tried for treason on the suspicion of plotting with Princess Elizabeth's servants. When Elizabeth herself succeeded to the throne, he became her astrologer.

Elizabeth consulted him about her "most grievous pangs and pains caused by toothache and the rheum", and about world geography. When she visited his house on the Thames at Mortlake she was shown his famous magic glass. In 1577 she called him to Windsor where for three days he explained and speculated to her about an alarming new comet.

Dee said that his evil reputation as a magician was the result of a clever production he staged at Cambridge of a play by Aristophanes in which the character Scarabaeus was made to fly up to Jupiter's palace with "a man and his basket of victuals on her back". But he hardly discouraged this reputation. He went into partnership with one Edward Kelly and the two of them claimed that their respective crystal globes would present apparitions and even make sounds. Dee's globe, and his magic glass (in fact highly polished coal), are preserved at the British Museum. Kelly always wore a black skull-cap to hide his missing ears which he had lost in the pillory, a fact Dee seems never to have known.

Dee was also in demand by impoverished European princes who hoped he would revive their fortunes by discovering the philosophers' stone. For this he searched indefatigably but unsuccessfully, though he was reported to have found a large quantity of the Elixir among the ruins of Glastonbury Abbey.

While he was away in Bohemia, the mob destroyed his Mortlake house with its fine library and on his return he suffered great poverty, only temporarily relieved by his appointment as Warden of Manchester College, Manchester. Though nominally the parson of two country parishes, he probably considered these chiefly as a source of income. For a time he lost much of the remuneration from them because he was too busy devising a reformed calendar to remember to fix the archbishop's Great Seal to his dispensation to hold them.

John Aubrey wrote of Dee: "He had a very fair clear sanguine complexion, a long beard as white as milke . . . He was a great peacemaker; if any of the neighbours fell out, he would never lett them alone till he had made them friends . . . The children dreaded him because he was accounted a conjurer."

Frederick William Densham
Warleggan, Cornwall

Soon after his appointment in 1931 to the living of Warleggan, a remote hamlet on Bodmin Moor, Frederick Densham (1869-1953) surprised a neighbour by asking whether he could hire a living-in gardener for a penny a year, plus free potatoes. He outraged his parishioners by painting the inside of his church red, blue and black, and though the bishop ordered him to repaint it white at his own expense, the blue and black still show through the whitewash. His congregation dwindling, he took to propping cardboard and wooden images in his church pews. In his Register of Services he recorded the weather and the behaviour of his two church stoves.

Round his rectory Densham erected an eight-foot barbed wire fence inside which he kept six to twelve Alsatians and other savage dogs. Tradesmen left what he needed in a box at the garden gate and the only person known to have penetrated to the rectory was an organist who had answered an advertisement. Locked in his rectory bedroom at night, the organist climbed out of the window and, avoiding the dogs, escaped over the wire. When a parishioner suggested that he should have a woman to help him in the house Densham replied that it was impossible since he kept fifty gallons of paraffin in his basement which she might set alight. He marked the chimneys of his rectory on the outside, so that if he was in his garden and there was a fire, he would know which room was ablaze.

The novelist Daphne du Maurier made two attempts to visit this disturbed man. On the first she was frightened away by the dogs. On the second, looking through the wire with a friend, she saw the rector "pacing up and down . . . in a dark frockcoat green with age, a black shovel hat upon his head". When they called out he raised his head to stare, then strode away.

Densham held his last services on January 18th 1953 and reported in the register that he had preached on

"Levelheadedness" to a congregation of five, which included reporters from *Life* and the *Western Daily Mail*. Some days later, when he had not been seen about, his parishioners broke into the rectory where they found the place "littered with paper and wood shavings", the floorboards torn up for fuel and Densham dead on the stairs. Since then there has been no resident rector. The rectory has been renamed The Rookery, after the second biggest rookery in Cornwall which is sited in its trees.

Joseph Dornford
Plymtree, Devon

Joseph Dornford (1794-1867) led an adventurous life before he was ordained. In 1811, aged seventeen, while still at Trinity College, Oxford, he enlisted as a rifleman in the Rifle Brigade and went to fight in the Peninsular War. It was suggested that he had been jilted in love, but the true reason according to Mozley, his successor at Plymtree, was that "he would rather fly to the ends of the earth and seek the company of cannibals or wild beasts than be bound to a life of tea and twaddle".

Back at Oxford, Dornford went during a vacation to climb Mont Blanc. He slipped and dragged three guides into a crevasse from which they never reappeared. When rescued he was found on his knees at the crevasse's edge, thanking God for his escape.

As a fellow of Oriel College, he was known among undergraduates as "the Corporal". He was still unmarried, and adopted towards women an attitude of extreme gallantry. "Possibly he had witnessed the havoc done by recruiting sergeants on the hearts of barmaids." At Moreton Pinkney, where he now held the living as "Perpetual Curate" this gallantry made him popular with his female parishioners but less so with his male ones. At Plymtree, Devon, where he went next to be rector, his chief antagonist suggested that "If Mr Dornford would get a missus of his own it would be better for he and better for we."

His choir, joining in the conflict, began to encroach more and more with their anthem on the time allowed for his sermon. One Sunday he took the opportunity of a pause in their singing to exclaim in a warm tone "Enough of that", and began to preach. The choir walked out of the church and never returned. The candlesticks were stolen from the altar and youths of a disreputable family broke into his garden at night to vandalize his choice plants.

When a young woman visited him to sympathize, his enemies ambushed her and fired guns over the hedge, so terrifying her that she died a few days later, as did her two infant

children. Dornford had an elaborate tomb made for them with iron railings and "a long touching inscription", but it was found thirty years later to be full of water and all that could be discovered of the three bodies was "some shovelfuls of charred *débris* and a tangled mass which had once been a beautiful head of hair".

To commemorate his unsuccessful romantic courtships Dornford planted an avenue of seventeen cypresses in his garden. Eventually he settled into a quiet domestic marriage, and when Thomas Mozley arrived at Plymtree the cypresses had been replaced by rhododendrons.

Dornford's great ambition at Plymtree was to drive a pair of fine horses the thirteen miles from Exeter to his parsonage in an hour, though the best he achieved was an hour and two minutes. If farmers with their carts blocked his way he cursed them with a fluency which offended and astonished them, though not their labourers. His fierce driving caused an accident in which his gardener's thigh was broken but Dornford remained the man's hero, as he was to many of the village poor. When he died a couple of old servants kept his grave, and "no grave in the county was kept better or so often supplied with new flowers."

Stephen Duck
Byfleet, Surrey

Stephen Duck (1705-56) was an agricultural labourer from Wiltshire who began to educate himself by reading Milton with the help of a dictionary. Presently he wrote verses, which he usually destroyed, but he was patronized, first by "a young gentleman of Oxford", then by George II's Queen Caroline. She sent Duck's verses to Pope who, though he did not admire them, also helped him. To the annoyance of Pope's friends the queen gave Duck a pension and he married one of her staff.

By 1730 Duck's *Poems on Several Subjects* had run to ten editions and it was rumoured that he would become the next Poet Laureate, though he never did. A few years later he married Sarah Big, the queen's housekeeper at Kew, and became the keeper of the queen's library.

In 1746 he took Holy Orders and held the living of Byfleet from 1752. Four years later, however, in a fit of melancholy, he drowned himself in a trout stream behind the Black Lion pub at Reading.

Henry Bate Dudley
Bradwell on Sea, Essex

Henry Bate Dudley (1745-1824) held the living of Fambridge in Essex from his father's death, but he spent his time in London where he lived the life of a man of pleasure. In 1773 he was involved in a notorious affray in Vauxhall Gardens, and became known as "the Fighting Parson".

Journalism was his chief interest. He was one of the earliest editors of the *Morning Post*, but when in 1780 he quarrelled with colleagues he set

associated. He bought the right of presentation there in 1781 and during the next sixteen years claimed to have spent £28,000 on rebuilding the church and reclaiming and embanking the land. As a member of the local hunt he once helped to kill a fox on the chancel roof.

In 1797, however, when he presented himself to the living, as he believed he was entitled to do, he was opposed by the Bishop of London on the grounds of simony – he had once

up his own rival paper, the *Morning Herald*. Soon afterwards he spent twelve months in Southwark prison for libelling the Duke of Richmond.

Dudley never took up the living of Bradwell with which he is chiefly

held a curacy at Bradwell. As soon as this matter was settled, it was found that the right of presentation had lapsed to the Crown. Dudley went to law but lost his case and the chaplain-general of the army was appointed instead.

Edward Eggington
Wednesbury, Staffordshire

Edward Eggington (d. 1744), vicar of Wednesbury from 1719 to 1744, was at the centre of the violent anti-Methodist riots which began there in 1743. Eggington had at first befriended John Wesley, but after another Methodist, Mr Williams, a Welshman, had "vilified the clergy and called them dumb dogs that could not bark", and two Methodists, a bricklayer and a plumber from London, had preached to such effect that the people "fell down in fits, and made strange hideous noises", Eggington preached against the Methodists the most wicked sermon that Wesley had ever heard.

In June the same year the united mobs of Darlaston, Walsall and Bilston smashed the windows of most of the Methodists' houses in Wednesbury, Darlaston and West Bromwich, broke their furniture and beat their pregnant women with clubs. In all eighty homes were wrecked. When the magistrate was called he "swung his hat round his head and cried 'Huzza!'" Wesley travelled to their help, but was seized and marched to two local magistrates who each in turn refused to see him and rioting continued till October.

Early next year Eggington required all Methodists to sign a paper declaring "that they would never read, or sing, or pray together, or hear the Methodist parsons any more". Those who signed were made to pay a penny to help make the rabble drunk. Those who did not, again had their houses wrecked. The rioting lasted six days and was worse than the previous year's. One man cut Mary Turner's Bible into fragments with his axe. Eggington died the same month.

Peter Charles Edward Elers
Thaxted, Essex

In 1976, at the age of forty-six, Peter Elers (b. 1930), vicar of Thaxted (where the Rev Conrad Noel had previously outraged parishioners by his Christian Socialism), agreed to become president of the Gay Christian Movement. In the autumn of that year he blessed two lesbian couples in his church. The Bishop of Colchester, who had until that time given Elers his support, now dissociated himself from this action, and Elers agreed not to repeat it.

William Elford
Lew Trenchard, Devon

William Elford (1754-1835), rector of Lew Trenchard from 1786 to 1833, lived nine miles away at Tavistock. When asked by his bishop why he did not live at Lew Trenchard he replied, "How can I live in a place where there is no barber to trim my wig?"

Instead he employed a curate, the Rev Caddy Thomas, who, to eke out his meagre income, took a resident pupil. When one day the gardener heard screams and the sound of heavy blows coming from the library he found Thomas battering the head of his pupil with the handle of a clasp knife. The gardener locked Thomas in his study, washed the blood from the student's head and took him home on horseback.

Elford was a notorious absentee and pluralist, also holding a curacy at Coryton and the vicarage of North Petherwyn, Cornwall.

Henry Thomas Ellacombe
Clyst St George, Devon

Henry Ellacombe (1790-1885), who held the living of Clyst St George on the Devon coast for thirty years from 1855, was a genealogist, a botanist and a campanologist. His garden contained 5,000 different plants, many of them exotic. He published a definitive book on the church bells of his county, listing their sizes, tones, quality, dates and legends. When collecting material he went about suitably dressed, running up every tower in Devonshire, often without permission.

The bells of one church are missing from his book because the incumbent took offence and excluded him. At ninety-three Ellacombe was described as "a very short man, very much bowed by age, with a white beard reaching half way to the ground, a pair of bright eyes and a good clear ringing voice".

Richard William Enraght
Bordesley, Bedfordshire

Richard Enraght (b. 1838), ritualist rector of Bordesley, offended the Low Church party by publishing a pamphlet in which he defended confession, prayers for the dead, the adoration of the Blessed Sacrament and the eastward position.

In 1880 he was imprisoned for forty-nine days in Warwick Gaol for refusing to conform to the Public Worship Regulations Act of 1874. Part of the case against him was that he had used wafer-bread which the Act forbade. A witness, hired for the purpose, had secreted a sample which he produced in court. "Happily Archbishop Tait intervened to put a stop to so outrageous a sacrilege, and insisted on the consecrated Particle being given up to him, subsequently consuming it with due reverence in his private chapel."

When Enraght's imprisonment was invalidated on technical grounds he returned to Bordesley, where for two years he persisted in his ritualistic practices, until the Bishop of Worcester forbade him to serve.

Frederick William Faber
Elton, Huntingdonshire

Frederick Faber (1814-63), poet and later Catholic priest, first took Holy Orders in the Church of England, and for two years held the living of the small parish of Elton.

At Oxford he had been slender and fair with an almost feminine grace. He was known as "Water-lily Faber" because of his poem, *The Cherwell Water-Lily*. He never married, and poems he wrote to young male friends, as well as his description of a tearful parting from a Greek boy who had been his servant during a five-week tour of the country, suggest homosexual leanings. On the other hand, when briefly a tutor in the Lake District, he wrote love poems to his employer's daughter, Dora Harrison, a girl of twelve. On hearing that Faber was to go into the Church, Wordsworth wrote, "I do not say you are wrong, but England loses a poet".

Faber early showed High Church leanings and, as a fellow of University College, Oxford, transformed his scout's hole into an oratory "to the great perturbation of that legitimate functionary". When he arrived at Elton the Methodists, who were strong there, crowded his church "ready to catch the Rector in his Romanism". He made a strange impression, preaching in a white surplice with black and red hood, walking about the village in a broad white choker and tall hat, and looking as if he fasted too much. At first he lived alone, cared for by seven servants, but gradually other young friends joined him and the rectory was transformed into a house of religious exercises, these sometimes lasting three hours. Faber and his friends began to think of themselves as monks and the rectory as their monastery; Faber's study became its oratory, smelling of cinnamon, a substitute for incense. In church he introduced the observance of saints' days and the hearing of confessions. Finally in 1845 he was received into the Catholic Church, following his hero Newman.

As rector of the Brompton Oratory, which he later became, Faber was important in the Romist revival of the mid-nineteenth century. He grew distressingly corpulent, but did not complain of his physical degeneration, and all who met him until his early death at forty-nine continued to find his personality strangely fascinating.

John William Fletcher
Madeley, Shropshire

John Fletcher (1729-85), the Swiss who became a friend of the Wesley brothers and a leading Methodist, had wished to be a soldier.

In England, where he came to learn the language, his patron, Thomas Hill of Tern Hall, Shropshire, enabled him to take Holy Orders as a "literate person" without attending an English university, then offered him the comfortable parish of Dunham in Cheshire, with an income of £400 a year and light duties. Fletcher rejected it and asked instead for the living of Madeley near Wellington in Shropshire, worth only half the amount and with two thousand irreligious colliers and forgemen for his parishioners.

When these claimed that they did not go to church on Sundays because they overslept he rose at five in the morning and walked round even the remotest parts of his parish, ringing a handbell. On evenings when they gathered for "dancing, drinking, revelling, and immorality and continued all night" he would burst into the room and "rebuke the thoughtless revellers with holy indignation". Thus, and by his attempts to suppress Madeley Wake, he aroused much hostility.

Like many Methodists, Fletcher also angered other clergy by preaching in their parishes. When he opened a meeting house at Madeley Wood its parson fastened a notice to the church door accusing Fletcher of "rebellion, schism, and being a disturber of the public peace".

In 1781, at the late age of fifty-two he returned there and married the Methodist Mary Bosanquet, but died of typhus four years later. He lies buried in Madeley churchyard.

Henry Fowler
Minchin Hampton, Gloucestershire

Henry Fowler (1583-c.1644) of Minchin Hampton was treated with more than typical brutality by Parliamentarian soldiers during the Civil War, though there is no record of his sequestration. On New Year's Day, 1643, one of a party which had come to his house "took him by the throat and held the point of his sword to his breast, two more presented their pistols to him, another shook his pole-axe over his head, and others beat him with their pole-axes, railing at him for reading Common Prayer and His Majesty's proclamation; calling him 'mass-priest', 'rogue', 'rascal', with other contumelious language." Though he was sixty-two and already lame, they knocked him down and so beat him that he was a cripple for the rest of his life – all this in the presence of his wife and children who prayed on their knees for mercy while friends of the Parliamentarian captain stood around jeering and clapping their hands.

Edward Drax Free
Sutton, Lincolnshire

Edward Free (1765-1843), rector of Sutton near Lincoln, was found guilty in 1829 of numerous offences, including taking the lead from the roof of his church, grazing cattle and swine in his churchyard, using profane language, possessing indecent prints and books, drunkenness and having illicit connections with a number of maid servants. He was sentenced to be deprived of his living.

Langton Freeman
Bilton, Warwickshire

Langton Freeman (1710-84), rector of Bilton in Warwickshire, lived twelve miles away in the manor house at Whilton in Northamptonshire, riding to Bilton on Sundays to hold services. He was a bachelor of notorious meanness, who would beg lunches from working men and pilfer the larders of richer friends. However in his will he left repayments to those he had robbed. He also left instructions that his body should be carried in his bed into his garden summer-house, which was to be locked up, fenced off and planted around with evergreens. In return for keeping it in this condition he left his nephew the manor house.

Seventy-five years later, when the summer-house had become dilapidated and the trees had been cut down, Freeman's body was found inside, "a dried up skinny figure, having apparently the consistence of leather, with one arm laid across his chest, and the other hanging down the body, which, though never embalmed, seems to have remained perfectly uncorrupted."

John Froude
Knowstone, Devon

John Froude (1777-1853) was the twelfth child and only son of John Froude senior. In 1804 he succeeded his father as vicar of Knowstone. At this time – when at least twenty clergymen in the diocese of Exeter each kept their own packs of hounds – Froude became notorious. The bishop, Henry Phillpotts, summoned him to answer the charges made against him in sundry articles in the *Western Times*, commonly headed, "Knowstone Again". When Froude refused to answer Phillpotts' summons to Exeter, Phillpotts went to Knowstone.

On July 31st, 1831, he found "Mr Froude ill in bed. The church good; house fair; in dining room six fox's brushes, two of them bell-pulls with a fox engraved, and Tally-ho! upon them." This is no doubt the bishop's version of the occasion when Froude, warned by posted look-outs, arranged for his housekeeper to tell Phillpotts that he was suffering from typhus and the bishop left in a hurry. At once Froude put on his long gaiters and went hunting for the rest of the day.

Finally the bishop *did* interview Froude. It was a winter morning and Froude sat near the fire, apparently seriously ill and heavily wrapped. He ordered brandy and water "hot and strong for the Bishop". When Phillpotts refused and tried to question him, Froude interrupted, saying, "It's my only doctor, my lord, is a drop of brandy; and if I had but taken it when I got my chill, I shouldn't now be as I be, deaf as a haddock, and nursing this fire like an old woman." Ten minutes after the bishop had left Froude was again seen to set out on horseback with his hounds – remarking later that he did not expect further visits because the air of Knowstone was too keen for the bishop.

Froude had other feuds. One Sunday after morning service he made his curate drunk and had him hung in a sack from a beam in an outhouse. When the congregation arrived for Evensong there was no priest to take the service. The curate couldn't and Froude wouldn't. Froude also caused serious injury to a neighbouring baronet by selling him a horse, below the eyelids of which he had placed hemp seeds. The pain of the seeds bursting drove the horse wild and the baronet was thrown.

Froude was a close friend of the Rev Jack Russell, another Master of Foxhounds with his own pack. When a curate Russell hunted with Froude and wrote of him, "He had an old liver-coloured spaniel called Crack, a wide ranger, but under perfect command. He used to say he could hunt the parish with that dog from the top of the church tower. You could hear his view-halloo for miles; and his hounds absolutely flew to him when they heard it. Let me add, his hospitality knew no bounds."

Despite the many discreditable stories which have accumulated round Froude (often pronounced "Frowde" by outsiders but "Froode" by natives), his wife at his death called him "dear saint". He is buried in a vault below Knowstone church which has been much altered since his time. His rectory was damaged by fire and several times rebuilt so that only part of the stable walls remain. But the nearby church at Molland, where he also held the living, is still as he knew it, with the three-decker pulpit he used.

Thomas Fuller
Waltham Abbey, Essex

Thomas Fuller (1608-61), though a Royalist, survived without excessive hardship the turbulence of the Civil War and Commonwealth, only to die of a fever the year after the Restoration. He is best remembered for his massive *The Church History of Britain*, a book which he risked bringing up to the date of his own troubled times.

At first Fuller held the living of Broadwindsor, Dorset, where he began to publish his account of the Crusades, *History of the Holy Warre*. Here he was so popular as a preacher that he would have "one congregation listening in the church and

the other at the window". He claimed not to have been formally sequestered from this living, but nevertheless left it for London in 1641, and then, as he became increasingly suspect, moved to Oxford. His seventeen weeks at Oxford, he said, cost him more than seventeen years at Cambridge (where he had been educated), but he probably referred

to the books and possessions he had had to abandon in London.

Fuller next became chaplain to Sir Ralph Hopton, one of the king's more moderate generals. After Hopton's defeat he was at the siege of Basing House and much offended when the cannon of "those howling wolves" (the attackers) disturbed his studies in its fine library. After Basing House fell he went to Exeter and helped to arrange for the city's surrender.

In about 1648 he took the living of Waltham Abbey in Essex, where he continued to write his church history. The complete work was published in 1655, its various sections dedicated to different influential people. One of Fuller's enemies, Helyn, found 350 faults in the book and attacked the dedications, though these were in fact only an early form of publication financed by subscription. Another, South, described Fuller as "running round London with his big book under one arm and his little wife under the other . . . recommending himself as a dinner guest by his facetious talk". But he had many friends and it was they and his moderate political views which enabled him to survive successfully. When permitted at the Restoration to take up again the living he had abandoned at Broadwindsor he went to hear the new incumbent preach and decided that he deserved to stay there.

Fuller was one of the first to make a living by his writing and claimed that he never caused any of his publishers any loss. Sometimes he would write the first word of every line of a sheet and then fill up the spaces. He was reputed to have an astonishing memory, "repeating 500 strange names after two or three hearings". He died, "crying out for his pen and ink to the last". He is buried at Cranford near Hounslow.

Nathaniel Gill
Burgh, Norfolk

Nathaniel Gill (1606-69), a keen Royalist, was sequestered from his living of Burgh in 1643, but for the next seven years defiantly and remarkably remained there, continuing to baptise and marry his parishioners; he even kept the parish registers so the name of his Puritan replacement is unknown.

Eventually he was driven away to Bungay, still with the registers, but he returned to Burgh at the Restoration, when he made this entry: "Nath. Gill (after seventeen yeares of sequestration, by traytors, rebels, Anabaptists, Quakers and Presbyterians) was restored to his rectory of Burrough and preached on Christmasse day 1660." Later he also held the nearby living of Aylsham, but retained Burgh, where he was buried.

Bernard Gilpin
Houghton-le-Spring, County Durham

Bernard Gilpin (1517-83), vicar of Houghton-le-Spring, a vast northern parish including fourteen villages, would make annual pilgrimages through such remote areas as Ribbesdale and Tyndale, for which he became known as "the Apostle of the North". As he travelled he would give away his spare cash and even his clothes to those in need. Seeing a peasant's horse fall dead while ploughing, he told his servant to replace it with his own. He was so well liked that, on another oc-casion, a thief who learned that a horse he had stolen was Gilpin's, returned it.

In his large rectory Gilpin would entertain to dinner, on each Sunday from Michaelmas to Easter, all who cared to come, seating them in three divisions according to rank. In his parish he founded a grammar school and himself boarded twenty-four scholars in his vicarage.

But he had made Catholic enemies.

At first Bishop Turnstall defended him but when they took thirty-two articles of accusation to Bishop Bonner in London, Gilpin was summoned south to defend himself. On the way he broke a leg and by the time he could complete the journey Queen Mary had died.

Under Queen Elizabeth he was offered the bishopric of Carlisle, and the provostship of Queen's College, Oxford, but refused both, preferring to stay and work in his parish. He died of a genuine accident when, in Durham market, an ox escaped and trampled him to the ground.

Edward Girdlestone
Halberton, Devon

Edward Girdlestone (1805-84), who became known as "the Agricultural Labourer's Friend", held a number of West Country livings. At Halberton in Devon, where he moved in 1862, he preached against low wages to such effect that the farmers of the parish shouted him down at a vestry meeting, refused him a church rate and presented themselves in a body at the Wesleyan chapel. In response he organized a campaign of migration which sent between four and five hundred labourers and their families to the more prosperous North. The effect of this was to raise wages in Devon from seven or eight shillings a week in 1866 to seventeen shillings by 1870.

In 1868 at a meeting of the British Association in Norwich, Girdlestone

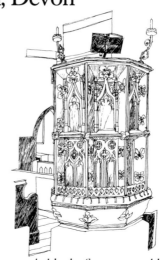

was probably the first to say publicly that agricultural labourers should have a union. He died of a cold, caught on the way to visit the Prince of Wales at Sandringham.

Thomas Goffe
East Clandon, Surrey

In 1620, when Thomas Goffe (1591-1629) came to his first and only living at East Clandon, he was already known as an orator and playwright. Three of his bombastic tragedies had been produced by the students

of Christ Church, Oxford, and *The Careless Shepherdess* performed before the king and queen at Salisbury.

Goffe was also known as a woman hater, but nine years later the widow of his predecessor at East Clandon persuaded him to marry her by pretending to fall in love with his preaching. She and her sons so persecuted him that he only survived marriage a few months. When some Oxford friends came to dine with him she "look'd upon them with an ill Eye, as if they had come to eat her out of house and home . . . (she wearing the Breeches)", at which they talked only in Latin and "laughed exceedingly", driving her from the table in tears.

A friend, Thomas Thimble, had warned Goffe against his marriage. Goffe's last words were "Oracle, Oracle, Tom Thimble". He is buried in the middle of the chancel of his East Clandon church, but has no memorial.

George Cornelius Gorham
Brampford Speke, Devon

In the mid-nineteenth century George Gorham (1790-1857) provoked a controversy, as abstract as any mediaeval theological discussion about angels and the point of a needle, which filled the public galleries of law courts, inspired the publication of over fifty books and pamphlets and drove H.E. Manning and Henry Wilberforce among others out of the Church of England.

The question (to much simplify) concerned "baptismal regeneration": did baptising a child *always* grant him regeneration or only *sometimes*? Henry Phillpotts, Bishop of Exeter, said *always*. Gorham said *sometimes*.

As vicar of St Just in Cornwall, Gorham had already differed with Phillpotts, who had objected to several of Gorham's proposed curates. When, in 1847, the Crown offered Gorham the living of Brampford Speke, meant as a less onerous parish for his declining years, Phillpotts cross-examined Gorham for nine days, requiring written answers to 149 questions, before concluding that he could not install him.

The law case which followed went against Gorham, but the Judicial

Committee of the Privy Council reversed the decision. It was this important result, in which the State had ruled on a matter of doctrine, that forced certain High Church Anglicans to defect to Rome, though it allowed Low Church Evangelicals to stay in the Church of England.

Phillpotts did not give up. He appealed unsuccessfully to three other courts, and wrote to the churchwardens of Brampford Speke instructing them to report any heresies in Gorham's preaching. But Gorham kept his living, dying there five years later.

He had much support for his case against Phillpotts. The balance of a public subscription raised to pay his legal expenses was used to buy him a silver tea service.

Though an obstinate man, Gorham was not an unintelligent one. At Cambridge he had won an essay prize and another for mathematics. One of a number of books he published was entitled *The History and Antiquities of Eynesbury and St Neots in Huntingdonshire and of St Neots in Cornwall with some remarks respecting the Saxon saints from whom these places derive their names.* He was a keen botanist and his herbarium was bought by the Marquis of Buckingham for a high price. During his few years at Brampford Speke he rebuilt the church.

Robert Graham
Bolingbroke-cum-Hareby, Lincolnshire

In the summer of 1940 Robert Graham (1890-1951), rector of the remote parish of Bolingbroke-cum-Hareby, rang his church bell, and as a consequence was sentenced to four weeks in prison. Defence regulations during the war prohibited the ringing of church bells except as a warning that a German invasion had begun. Graham appealed, claiming he did not know of the regulation and the sentence was lifted.

Matthew Griffith
Bladon, Oxfordshire

Matthew Griffith (*c.* 1599-1665) was given the living of Benet Sherehog by King Charles I but was sequestered and imprisoned in 1642. Next year he escaped to join the king at Oxford and later helped defend Basing House. When this was stormed in October 1645 his daughter so insulted the Roundheads that they killed her.

After the Restoration Griffith held the living of Bladon near Woodstock for five years, but died in the pulpit of his church when he broke a blood vessel while preaching.

William Grimshaw
Haworth, Yorkshire

As a young curate William Grimshaw (1708-63) "led a careless life", but he underwent a conversion. By the time he became the parson as "Perpetual Curate" of the remote Yorkshire parish of Haworth he was a committed Calvinist. A gigantic man, he was reputed to have only one pair of shoes and one shabby coat. At Soddens – not the parsonage later to become the home of the Brontë family – he would sleep in his stable to leave room in the house for needy guests. Throughout the North he was known as the mad parson of the Yorkshire moors.

One year he put a stop to the Haworth races by successfully calling for a cloudburst. He drove his parishioners to church, sometimes literally with a whip. Often he would leave church during the singing of the psalm to chase up any who were idling in the churchyard, street or alehouse in time for his sermon. A visitor once passing a public house on Sunday morning "saw several persons making their escape out of it, some jumping out of the lower windows, and some over a low wall; he was at first alarmed, fearing the house was on fire; but, upon inquiring what was the cause of the commotion, he was told that they saw the parson coming."

As a result he raised the communicants in his parish from twelve to 1,200 and attracted people from far away to hear him preach. Such was his success that he went, with and without invitation, to preach in many other parishes. John Wesley had decreed that after his own brother Charles he would be third in the Methodist succession.

Grimshaw died of a fever raging in the village, having refused to take flight as others who could afford to had done.

James Hackman
Wiveton, Norfolk

James Hackman, eighteenth-century vicar of Wiveton, lay in wait on April 7th 1779 outside Covent Garden Theatre for the Earl of Sandwich's mistress and shot her dead when she emerged. He was tried at the Old Bailey, found guilty and hanged at Tyburn.

At his trial he admitted to being a victim of insane love. He said he had been overcome by a moment of frenzy which had induced him to commit a deed he now deplored.

Stephen Hales
Teddington, Middlesex

Stephen Hales (1677-1761), of Teddington, was a conscientious parish priest and at the same time a scientist who is still respected today. He had livings in Somerset and Hampshire, but chose to live at Teddington where he held a curacy and where, typically, he ensured for the parish a wholesome water supply, recording that this would fill a two-quart vessel "in three swings of a pendulum . . . which pendulum was 39²/10 inches long from the suspending nail to the middle of the plumbet". He encouraged morality in his female parishioners by making them do public penance for "irregular behaviour". He argued against drink and wrote an anonymous pamphlet, *A Friendly Admonition to the Drinkers of Brandy*, which by 1807 had reached a sixth edition. To landowners he pointed out that drinkers lost their appetites and thus reduced the demand for agricultural produce.

ure. He was less convinced than his contemporaries that the blood's heat derived from friction between the blood and the walls of the blood vessels.

His best known invention was a method of artificial ventilation, which he persuaded the French to fit to prisons in which they were holding English prisoners. In England the same system at the Savoy and Newgate prisons greatly reduced the numbers of prisoners who died.

Pope described Hales as a worthy and good man, though Horace Walpole called him a poor, good, primitive creature. Another friend noticed that he forgave those who offended him "not from want of discernment or sensibility" but as if considering them to be failed scientific experiments which "could therefore be calmly and dispassionately laid aside".

Hales read many papers on botany and physiology to the Royal Society, of which he became a fellow in 1718. From these his important book, *Statical Essays*, was compiled. In botany he was particularly concerned with the evaporation of water from plants, and in physiology with blood press-

He was befriended by Frederick, Prince of Wales, father of George III, who was fond of surprising him in his laboratory at Teddington. Frederick's widow put up a monument to Hales in Westminster Abbey, but he was buried below his own church tower at Teddington.

Charles Sawkins Harrison
Cottisford, Oxfordshire

Charles Harrison was rector at Cottisford in north Oxfordshire for forty-three years from 1853 onwards. Flora Thompson, in *Lark Rise to Candleford*, calls him Mr Ellison, rector of Fordlow.

"He was a parson of the old school", she writes; "a commanding figure, tall and stout, with white hair, ruddy cheeks and an aristocratically beaked nose, and he was as far as possible from the lambs of his flock. He spoke to them from a great height, physical, mental and spiritual. 'To order myself lowly and reverently before my betters' was the clause he underlined in the Church Catechism, for had he not been divinely appointed pastor and master to those little rustics." The other theme of his sermons was the duty of regular churchgoing. "He would hammer away at that for forty-five minutes, never seeming to realize that he was preaching to the absent."

When visiting his parishioners Harrison would "never mention religion.

That was looked upon in the parish as one of his chief virtues, but it limited the possible topics of conversation. Apart from his autocratic ideas, he was a kindly man, and he had come to pay a friendly call, hoping, no doubt, to get to know and to understand his parishioners better. But the gulf between them was too wide."

Joseph Harrison
Sustead, Norfolk

Joseph Harrison, vicar of Sustead in the 1630s, was brought before Archbishop William Laud's High Commission, accused of being so drunk he could not read Divine Service. He was also said to have conducted secret marriages, secretly baptised illegitimate children, associated with beggars, tinkers and bedlam men, and been abusive to the Bishop of Lichfield. All these charges were proved and he was deprived of his living, fined fifty pounds, sent to prison and excommunicated. A further charge that he practised magic and charmed pigs did not succeed.

William Harrison
Radwinter, Essex

William Harrison (1543-93), who held the living of the small Essex parish of Radwinter from 1559 till he died in 1593, was a Puritan, though not an extreme one. He is best remembered for his book, *A Description of England*. In it he makes many complaints about the state of the country. About lay patrons he writes that they "doo bestow advowsons of benefices upon their bakers, butlers, cookes, good archers, and housekeepers instead of other recompense". But he approved of the "comlie" dress of his fellow clergy compared with that of popish times when "to meet a priest . . . was to behold a peacocke that spreadethe his taile when he danseth before the henne". In 1583 his writing was considered sufficiently subversive for three ministers to be hanged for "dispensing Browne's books and Harrison's books".

Though Harrison's garden at Radwinter was "little above 300 foot of ground, such hath bene my good lucke in purchase of the varietie of simples, that notwithstanding my small abilitie, there are verie neere three hundred of one sort and other conteined therein, no one of them being common or usuallie to bee had." At the cost of twenty shillings his wife, Marion, and their maid would brew him 200 gallons of beer.

He was also a collector of Roman coins, and an enemy of local lawyers. In his will he left forty shillings to the poor of Radwinter.

Robert Stephen Hawker
Morwenstow, Cornwall

By the 1860s R.S. Hawker (1803-75) was well known as a poet and an eccentric. Parties would come from Bude to his remote parish of Morwenstow on the north Cornish coast to try to glimpse his strange figure in maroon coat and seaman's boots. From some he hid, some he sent to see the church, for others who had come on foot he refused to find a carriage home. Tennyson he questioned "in the coldest manner" until sure that it was the genuine poet. As soon as he died his fellow West Country parson, Sabine Baring-Gould, wrote his biography.

From his youth Hawker had enjoyed practical jokes. At Stratton, where his father was a clergyman, he persecuted three old ladies by having local tradesmen deliver unordered goods to them. When they received a coffin they left for Plymouth. Starting at a Stratton shop, he unravelled a ball of twine, tying up the village in a vast knot so that "people passin' along was pitched on their noses without zackly knowin' why."

At nineteen, while still at Oxford, he married Charlotte I'ans, a spinster of forty-one. Certainly they loved each other, but she brought him a useful annuity of £200 a year.

At Morwenstow, where he went in 1835 and stayed for the rest of his life, and where there had not been a resident parson for a hundred years, Hawker built a vicarage in the deep valley below the church, choosing a place where the sheep sheltered. He was not an architect and used T. F. Hunt's *Designs for Parsonage Houses*, but the frugality the author intended is not well represented by Hawker's substantial Victorian-Gothic building. It stands today, little changed though no longer the vicarage, still topped with four chimneys in the form of church towers which Hawker had known (Oxford, Stratton, Whitstone and North Tamerton) and a fifth modelled on his mother's tomb.

With his seaboots and maroon coat Hawker would wear a pink hat without a brim, not unlike a fez, and a fisherman's jersey, sewn into one side of which was a red cross to mark the place where the centurion's spear entered Christ's body. But in church he would dress splendidly, for example in magnificent purple velvet cope, white alb, stole richly embroidered in gold, green and amber chasuble and scarlet gloves. It was his habit to roam around the chancel out of sight beyond the rood screen, "reading now in English, now in Latin. At certain points . . . he would prostrate himself on the ground before the altar, with outstretched arms in the form of a cross."

A traditionalist, he refused to have his church re-roofed in slate, but instead had it re-shingled in oak. He forced the workmen engaged in this holy task to attend his services – and for the rest of his life was troubled by their poor workmanship. He also had the lower panels removed from his pulpit, on the grounds that the congregation should be able to see his feet, but he retained the narrow winding approach stairs and small gate, perhaps to enable him to whisper to visiting preachers as they descended backwards, "It is the strait and narrow way and few there be that find it." He hated box pews and called the owner of one of these to church to watch him destroy it with an axe in front of the owner's eyes. Above all he abominated Methodists, considering them the cause of the immorality in his parish, where few women came to the altar to be married unless compelled by pregnancy.

Knowing well the poverty of both farmers and labourers, and the importance to them of a good harvest, he was possibly the first to hold annual Harvest Festival services.

On the cliff top a short way from his church he built a hut (it is still there) from the timbers of wrecked ships; here he spent many hours reading, writing and contemplating. The wrecks he sometimes saw from the hut – there were eighty-one around Bude between 1825 and 1875 – provided him with his most unpleasant duty, the burying of the drowned. These were often so damaged by the sharp rocks that they were limbless. In 1859 five out of seven bodies from one wreck had no heads. The figurehead of the *Caledonia*, wrecked off Morwenstow in 1842, stands in the churchyard above the grave of the captain.

Hawker loved animals. At North Tamerton where he was briefly a curate before coming to Morwenstow, he kept a tame pig called Gyp which went parish visiting with him. At Morwenstow he had nine cats, which often followed him to church and cavorted in the chancel. He excommunicated one for catching a mouse on Sunday. He also kept two deer, named Robin Hood and Maid Marian. Robin Hood once felled a visiting Low Church clergyman, who had to be released by Hawker from Robin Hood's horns.

He was also fond of strong tea – Twining's Souchong or Congou – making it by filling the pot with leaves and pouring water into the crevices. He was a heavy smoker and would carry with him to his hut a basketful of charged pipes. But he hated beards, and above all false teeth, which he believed were taken from corpses.

He suffered great distress when his first wife died, but quickly married again, a half Polish girl, forty years his junior. At this time he was already taking opium, and though he gave it up during the early years of his happy second marriage, he returned to it. His most inspired poem, *The Quest of the Sangraal*, owes many of its visionary lines to the habit. His best known poem, *Song of the Western Men*, was published while he was at Oxford. Trelawny, its imprisoned hero, was Sir John Trelawny, held in the Tower by James I in 1628.

Hawker was formally converted to Catholicism twelve hours before he died, thus causing a scandal. His biographer Baring-Gould claimed that this was a last-minute aberration, engineered by his wife when his mind was feeble, but he had more probably been a secret Catholic for many years.

John Hencher
Amblecote, Worcestershire

John Hencher (b. 1931), vicar of Amblecote near Stourbridge from 1964 to 1970, advertised in a 1966 issue of the *Worcester Diocesan Messenger* in these words: "I would like a nice cosy wife. If anyone would like to take me on, I'd be glad to hear from them. She must adore Shakespeare and be prepared to sleep in a four-poster bed." When many hopeful applicants called at his fifteen-bedroom vicarage he went into hiding and admitted that he had chosen a mistaken and risky way to obtain the wife for whom he wished.

John Stevens Henslow
Hitcham, Suffolk

While retaining his Hitcham living, John Henslow (1796-1861) held Cambridge professorships in mineralogy then botany. Among many books, he published a standard work on the flora of Suffolk. He identified the plants which the children of the school found in his parish and by 1860 had recorded 406 species. In 1960, sixty of these could no longer be found.

Henslow refused the position of naturalist on the *Beagle*'s voyage of exploration, but suggested instead his ex-pupil from Cambridge, Charles Darwin. At home, he received the specimens which were sent back from the *Beagle*.

He was interested in many other sciences, including chemistry, entomology, conchology and archaeology. He invented artificial fertilizers which were still being manufactured in Ipswich a hundred years after his death.

In the hungry 1840s he let allotments on his glebe land. Local employers were so angered that, at a vestry meeting, they agreed to hire no labourer who rented an allotment. In response, Henslow let fifty-two, and at the time of his death had so far overcome opposition that 150 were being cultivated in the village. He is buried in Hitcham churchyard.

George Herbert
Fugglestone-with-Bemerton, Wiltshire

George Herbert (1593-1633) was well born and expected to follow a career at court, where he was favoured by James I, but his own ill health and the king's death so affected him that he changed his mind and took Holy Orders. About this change of life he wrote: "the domestic servants of the King of Heaven should be of the noblest families on earth." Although the time had made "the sacred name of priest contemptible", he would labour to make it honourable.

In 1630, with the encouragement of Bishop William Laud, he took the living of Fugglestone-with-Bemerton, near Salisbury. Here he lived a holy life, devoting his time to writing, and to his parish duties. He was so loved in his parish that, according to Izaak Walton, ploughmen would stop ploughing when they heard "Mr Herbert's saints-bell" and pray for him before starting work again.

He died after less than three years at Bemerton from consumption, and is buried below the church's altar. During his last illness he wrote *The Temple; or Sacred Poems and Private Ejaculations* and *A Priest to the Temple, or the Countrey Parson His Character and Rule of Holy Life*. Both were published after his death. King Charles I, during his imprisonment before his execution, sustained his spirits by reading George Herbert's poems.

Robert Herrick
Dean Prior, Devon

Robert Herrick (1591-1674), the poet, was vicar of Dean Prior near Ashburton, first from 1629 to 1647 when he was ejected, then again after the Restoration, from 1662 to 1674. At Dean Prior he professed to long for London and to be bored with "lothed" and "dull" Devon.

He described his parishioners as "rude almost as rudest savages" and once threw his sermon at them for failing to listen. But he was kind to them and fed the poor. When his maid died he wrote of her:

In this little Urne is laid
Prewdence Baldwin (once my maid)
From whose happy spark here let
Spring the purple violet.

Herrick farmed his ninety-three acre glebe, kept a pet lamb, a cat, a goose, a cock, a hen and a spaniel called Tracy, and taught one of his pigs to drink from a pint tankard. His poems were forgotten for over a hundred years until Nichols wrote about them in the *Gentleman's Magazine* of 1796-7.

John Hodgson
Jarrow, Durham

John Hodgson (1779-1845), rector of Jarrow from 1808 to 1833 and author of a laborious *History of Northumberland*, played an important part in the development of the Davy safety lamp for mining. When Sir Humphry Davy visited Newcastle in 1815 Hodgson explained to him the problem of lighting mines, where accumulations of methane gas (fire-damp) were easily set alight by a naked flame and could cause frightful explosions. Later Hodgson sent Davy a bottle of fire-damp to London to test his experiments, in which Davy enclosed the flame of a lamp inside a gauze screen.

In 1816 Davy sent his first two lamps to Hodgson, who took one down Hebburn pit and walked about in "a terrible atmosphere of fire-damp", greatly alarming the miners he met who believed it to be a candle.

Reynolds Hole
Caunton, Nottinghamshire

Reynolds Hole (1819-1904), who became the country's best known authority on roses, had literary inclinations when young. "Enter a man swimming for his life" is the first line of a drama he wrote at the age of eight. At ten he wrote poetry, mostly during dull sermons. At eighteen, while still at Newark Grammar School, he edited his own paper, the *Newark Bee*. Later he attended the Wednesday lunches of *Punch* contributors and became the close friend of the illustrator John Leech.

In 1850 Hole became rector of Caunton, the village where he had lived since he was a few months old. Here, "sauntering in the garden one summer's evening with cigar and book", his eyes "rested on a rose" (d'Aguesseau *gallica*). From that moment roses obsessed him. Eventually he had four to five thousand rose trees in his garden and spreading over his father's garden and farm. He wrote *A Book About Roses*, and was largely responsible for the First National Rose Show of 1858. His own roses won prizes throughout the country.

At the age of forty-one he married a girl twenty-one years his junior. He wrote to his sister, "She is rather young, 20 yrs (I have spoken to her

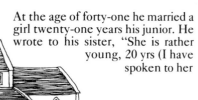

seriously concerning this delinquency, and note improvement)."

But she had inherited a useful £9,000 and he was passionately fond of her. When she was away from home he headed his letters "The Deserted Village" and addressed her as "Deliciousest Ownums". Their only son he called "that Tweet".

In 1887 Hole became Dean of Rochester, and five years later, now weighing seventeen stone, involved himself in controversy by defending the playing of whist for small stakes and modest drinking. In reply the teetotaller W. Kempster wrote a pamphlet entitled *The Dean and the Drink*. Hole died aged eighty-four and is buried at Caunton.

Richard Hooker
Bishop's Bourne, Kent

In 1579 Richard Hooker (1554-1600), a moderate Puritan, was suspended from Corpus Christi College, Oxford, probably because he fell into disfavour with its vice-president, the ardent Puritan John Barfoot. Two years later, now living in London, he married Joan Churchman, the daughter of his landlord, described as "an ill-tempered woman, neither rich nor beautiful". Returning to London in 1585, he became Master of the Temple. This appointment infuriated the extreme Puritan lecturer, Walter Travers, who caused violent scenes at the Temple church.

In 1595 Hooker obtained the living of Bishop's Bourne near Canterbury.

By this time his great eight-volume defence of Anglicanism, *Ecclesiastical Polity*, had begun to be published and its fame brought him many visitors there.

Hooker lived a holy life, one of his habits being to lock himself into his church for many hours on Fridays and other fast days. His biographer, Izaak Walton, describes him at this time as "usually girt in a coarse gown or canonical coat; of a mean stature, and stooping . . . of so mild and humble a nature, that his poor parish clerk and he did ever talk but with both their hats on, or both off, at the same time." He died, after only five years at Bishop's Bourne, "meditating on the number and nature of the angels".

Although both Thomas Fuller and Izaak Walton suggest that Hooker's wife was shrewish and extravagant – Walton describing her as like a "dripping house" – she failed to impoverish him, since he left £1,092 9s 2d in his will. Her bad name is probably the work of two of Hooker's pupils at Oxford, one of whom, Edwin Sandys, was later involved in litigation with Joan Hooker's daughter.

Michael Hudson
Uffington, Lincolnshire

Michael Hudson (*c.*1605-48), rector of Uffington and Royal Chaplain, guided King Charles I in his escape from Oxford to Newcastle in 1646. Hudson himself then fled to Sandwich in an attempt to reach France, but was arrested and sent to the Tower. He escaped disguised as an apple seller, raised a troop of Royalists and seized Woodcroft House in Northamptonshire.

Hudson died in the subsequent siege. Having surrendered, but finding himself nevertheless about to be killed, he threw himself over the battlements "and hung by the hands as intending to fall into the moat beneath, till they cut off his wrists and let him drop, and then ran down to hunt him in the water, where they found him paddling with his stumps, and barbarously knocked him on the head." When he was dead "one Walker, a chandler, cut out his tongue, and carried it about the country as a trophy."

Dr Rochecliffe, in Walter Scott's novel *Woodstock* is based on Hudson.

George Hustler
English Bicknor, Gloucestershire

George Hustler (1827-1905) was a keen hunting man all his life. He first held the living of Stillingfleet, seven miles from York, then moved to the family home of Ackland. But the generosity of his life style in this large house forced him to move again and in 1877 he took the Gloucestershire living of English Bicknor.

In this parish he built his own kennels. He hunted deer and fox in the Forest of Dean and was also a keeper and judge of prize poultry. His household was notably unpunctual. Guests who sat down to lunch at one would sometimes not be fed until a quarter to three. When his family were not looking he would give away his best garments to those in need.

When out hunting at the age of seventy-seven on a horse called

Macaroni he died of a heart attack. Both he and his wife lie buried in English Bicknor churchyard.

Leonard James
Rokeland, Norfolk

On Twelfth Night, 1608, Leonard James, who had been rector of Rokeland for the previous twenty-seven years, was barbarously murdered with his wife's consent by his curate, Mr Lane. Lane was hanged and Mrs James burned at the stake.

Samuel Johnson
Corringham, Essex

Samuel Johnson (1649-1703), obstinate rector of Corringham and implacable enemy of popery, was found guilty in 1683 of seditious libel, fined 500 marks and sent to prison. A sermon he had preached before the Lord Mayor of London was formally burned by the hangman.

After his release he published further tracts against popery but was again arrested when he addressed one of them to "Protestants in the Present Army". Once more he was fined 500 marks and in addition sentenced to be degraded, to stand four times in the pillory and to be whipped from Newgate to Tyburn.

The degradation was improperly carried out, since he was not stripped of his cassock. Nevertheless he stood in the pillory as ordered and during his whipping received 317 strokes with a whip of nine knotted cords. James II, when asked to intervene, said that since Mr Johnson had the spirit of martyrdom, it was fit that he should suffer. Johnson's spirit remained unbroken, his reputation was enhanced, and when a new rector was sent to Corringham, the parishioners refused to admit him.

While still being treated for his whipping, Johnson published a further anti-papal tract, but the revolution of 1688 saved him and all judgements against him were revoked. He did not, however, receive from William III the bishopric he thought he deserved and only much later was granted a bounty of £1,000 and a pension of £300.

Morgan Jones
Blewbury, Berkshire

John Keble, father of the better known John Keble of Hursley, held two livings, to one of which, Blewbury on the Berkshire downs, he appointed Morgan Jones, the notorious miser, as curate in 1781. At first Jones lived in lodgings and grew corpulent, but once he moved into his parsonage, his miserly instincts developed. During his whole forty-three years at Blewbury he wore the same coat and hat. When the black hat collapsed he replaced its brim with a brown one from a scarecrow. His coat was so patched and darned that it was reduced to the size of a jacket. For many years after he died a parishioner preserved it in a glass case.

Jones kept a store of unused shirts and wore a single one the whole time, except in bed or if he needed to mend it. When this had been similarly patched for many years it became "too short to reach down to his small-clothes", so he added part of a previously abandoned shirt, collar frill downwards. Growing absent-minded in old age, he sometimes conducted funerals in this garment, the rest of his clothes tied together with string.

He lived on 2s 6d a week, cooked only on Sundays and bought only two necessities (bread and bacon) and one luxury (tea). To obtain the bacon he went three times to a farmer – once to order, once to collect and once to pay – timing each visit so that he would be given tea and supper. He drank only sugarless and milkless tea. He had once been exceedingly fond of ale and used to "partake too freely". When he drank too much at a wedding and this was talked about, he promised never to touch ale again and kept his promise.

He wrote a thousand sermons but never had them printed because he would not risk the postage to offer them to a publisher. For paper he used the backs of old marriage licences, scraps of brown paper, grocer's paper or even the backs of sheets of sandpaper. But he was known to give generously to charities and contributed, for example, to the Society for the Conversion of Jews. Furthermore he was a peaceable and well-liked parson.

When Jones retired in 1824, he hoped to live at Blewbury, but could find no family to keep him free, so he returned to little known relatives in his native Wales. They were well satisfied with the £18,000 in his will.

William Jones
Broxbourne, Hertfordshire

William Jones (1755-1821), curate and then vicar of Broxbourne for forty years, kept a diary in which he recorded his struggle against poverty. He would add up his expenditure for a quarter (£36), and realize that it was twice his income. His whole wardrobe, he reckoned, was worth less than twelve shillings. He deplored his own "scurvy . . . filthy and worse than beastly practice" of snuff-taking which cost him three guineas a year. When he finally gave it up he wrote ". . . huzza! huzza! for I have hitherto succeeded beyond my tip-top expectations. My poor, grumbling nose has kept a complete fast since the last date!! In all this time . . . my snuff box has not been, for many minutes together, forgotten. It may therefore be truly supposed that I have been in a sort of *snuffy* purgatory. And my *hands* have not been idle, for again, and again, have they involuntarily been rummaging all my pockets, in search, I suppose, of my snuff box."

Jones had a great quarrel with a self-made farmer named Rogers, who persistently let his cattle into Jones's pastures, and tried to enclose part of the churchyard. When Jones was hoping to succeed to the living of Broxbourne he discovered that Rogers had written "a letter full of calumnies and misrepresentations"

to the bishop. Rogers's efforts failed, but on June 6th 1801, when the bell ringers of Broxbourne "were expressing their joy for my having been inducted, Rogers, on his return from Hertford market, *bottle-valiant*, dared to cut some of the ropes." Jones' supporters revenged themselves on Rogers "that night and many succeeding days and nights, not only by the ringing, but by hisses, hootings, and various insults of the populace."

He quarrelled, too, with his parsimonious wife, Theodosia, and kept *A Book of Domestic Lamentations* (now lost) in which he recorded their differences. She was "a lawyer's daughter and possessed such a wonderful volubility of speech, such a miraculous power of twirling and twisting every argument to her own interest that I am no match for her High Mightiness." Her grievances centred on their poverty and she regularly pressed him to continue taking pupils and to extract his tithes in full.

John Keble
Hursley, Hampshire

at eighteen he (and another student) became the first in the university since Robert Peel to obtain double first-class honours.

Thereafter he regularly refused positions of profit or influence, either from modesty or out of duty to his family.

The only important appointment he did hold was the Professorship of Poetry at Oxford, from 1831 to 1841. But the sermon he delivered on Assize Sunday, 1833, before the assize judges in St Mary's, Oxford, was more influential than any of his lectures, for the Oxford Movement was its direct result.

Keble became well known, however, for his book of religious poems, *The Christian Year*. He wanted to delay their publication until after his death, but he eventually agreed to an anonymous edition. When he did die, forty years later, ninety-five editions had been printed. The poems, many of them still well known as hymns, were so faulty in metre and construction that Wordsworth suggested he should help Keble to improve them.

At forty-four he married a wife who

For thirty years, from 1836 until his death, John Keble (1792-1866) led the simple life of a country parson in the village of Hursley, five miles from Winchester. Before then he held curacies in the three Gloucestershire villages of East Leach, Burthorpe and Southrop, where the total populations were a thousand and his income only £100 a year. Yet Newman wrote of him that he was "the true and primary author" of the Oxford Movement, and Liddon, the biographer of Pusey (who later became the movement's leader), says "when all else had been said and done, people would wait and see what came from Hursley before they made up their minds."

Keble was a brilliant child, educated solely by his father with such success that at fourteen he won a scholarship to Corpus Christi College, Oxford;

was an invalid – and himself came to his wedding with a broken collar bone. For the rest of his life he was forced continually to take her away for long periods of convalescence. When reading the lesson for the day to her, as she lay dying, he collapsed, paralysed in both legs, but when he recovered consciousness, insisted on returning to sit with her.

At Hursley he invited his parishioners to confess to him, seeing this as the best way to enforce discipline among them. On the other hand he encouraged and joined in Sunday cricket with them after Evensong, until this caused such an outcry that it was stopped. Though many of his friends, including Newman, Manning and Robert Wilberforce, were converted to Roman Catholicism, he, like Pusey, remained loyal to the Church of England, and his influence on the Oxford Movement grew when he became Pusey's confessor.

Keble is buried in Hursley churchyard and commemorated by a bust in Westminster Abbey, but his greatest memorial is Keble College, Oxford, designed by Butterfield and opened three years after his death to provide an education "in strict fidelity to the Church of England".

Robert Francis Kilvert
Clyro, Radnorshire

Until the publication of his diaries in 1939-40, Francis Kilvert (1840-79) had been forgotten. In the 1860s and 1870s he was a curate for seven years in the remote parish of Clyro on the Welsh borders; he then more briefly held livings at St Harmon and at Bredwardine in the same area, before dying of a burst appendix at the age of only thirty-eight. Once published, Kilvert's diaries were an instant success.

The diaries cover the years between 1870 and 1879 and tell with love and wonder of his parish life. His love was often specific, and he was affected by young girls, especially nubile brunettes. He would visit cottagers' wives when they were due to bath their little daughters so that he could watch.

He fell in love with one Daisy Thomas, but was rejected by her father. For this reason he left Clyro, and for a time helped his own father in his Wiltshire parish of Langley Burrell. Here he met Ettie Meredith-Brown, whose cheeks had the "dusky bloom and flush of a ripe pomegranate". Again the girl's parents ended the affair.

Returning to the Welsh borders, Kilvert presently married Elizabeth Rowlands, a homely girl, sixteen years his junior. They honeymooned in Scotland, and on their return were met by his parishioners who unharnessed the horses of the carriage and themselves dragged it to the doors of Bredwardine vicarage. A fortnight later Kilvert was dead.

The diaries came to his widow, who destroyed two sections, each of six months, one of which must have described their own courtship, the other his earlier affair with Ettie Meredith-Brown. Nor did Elizabeth

Kilvert want the remainder to be published, but a nephew of Kilvert's eventually sent them to William Plomer, who edited the 1,250,00 words down to 400,000 to make three volumes.

Kilvert's widow wanted to be buried beside him at Bredwardine, but by the time she died, thirty years later, both neighbouring spaces had been taken by maiden ladies, so she lies in the churchyard extension.

John King
Ashby de la Launde, Lincolnshire

John King (1793-1875), vicar of Ashby de la Launde, bred race horses which he entered for races as owned by "Mr Launde". Breeding was his interest and he was rarely to be seen on the racecourse itself. When, however, in 1874 his horse Apology won the One Thousand Guineas, The Oaks and the St Leger races, the Bishop of Lincoln wrote to King to suggest that he was neglecting his parish duties. King referred the bishop to his solicitors and informed him that there was no way the bishop could remove him from his living, so if he resigned it would "not be from . . . fear of any consequences". King died the next year, but Apology lived on to win the Ascot Cup in 1876.

Charles Kingsley senior
Barnack, Northamptonshire

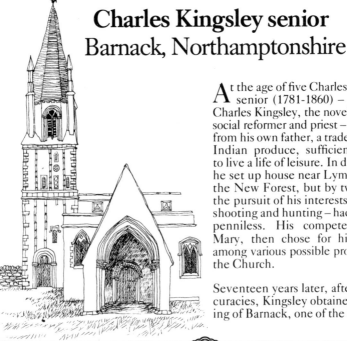

At the age of five Charles Kingsley senior (1781-1860) – father of Charles Kingsley, the novelist, poet, social reformer and priest – inherited from his own father, a trader in West Indian produce, sufficient money to live a life of leisure. In due course he set up house near Lymington in the New Forest, but by twenty-six the pursuit of his interests – chiefly shooting and hunting – had left him penniless. His competent wife, Mary, then chose for him, from among various possible professions, the Church.

Seventeen years later, after various curacies, Kingsley obtained the living of Barnack, one of the richest in

England (£1,200 per annum). Here, near the Fens, which at that time were undrained and abounded in wildlife, he could again indulge his passion for shooting.

Barnack's fourteenth-century rectory still survives, though it is no longer the home of the rector and has lost much of its land. In Kingsley's time it was known as the "Palace of Barnack"; it had several walled gardens, an orchard, a stableyard, a farmyard, enough land to be described as a park, and its own ghost. This character was known as "Button Cap" because, above his flowered dressing-gown, he wore a cap with a button on it. He chiefly haunted the Great North Room where he would turn over the leaves of books in search of a missing deed.

Kingsley left Barnack when he contracted the ague (malaria), common at that time in the Fens. A year later in 1831 he obtained the living of Clovelly, the picturesque North Devon fishing village which descends with such steepness to the Bristol Channel. Here he took an interest in his fishermen parishioners and their way of life. "He could steer a boat, hoist and lower sail, 'shoot' a herring net and haul a sein with the best of them and when the fishing fleet put to sea, whatever the weather, he would start off 'down street' to give a short service and join in the singing of the old Prayer Book version of the 121st Psalm:

Though storms be sudden, and waters deep
Thy Guardians will not sleep."

Kingsley was a strict father, compelling his son to come to his Barnack study to recite long passages of Latin and Greek. More profitably, he passed on to him his own skill as an artist, and at Clovelly, he encouraged his children to collect and identify the marine life of the shore.

In 1840 Kingsley left Clovelly for St Luke's, Chelsea, needing to return to a rich living to help pay for the private education of his sons; here he remained for the next twenty years. He died at the Chelsea rectory and is buried in Brompton Cemetery.

Charles Kingsley
Eversley, Surrey

Charles Kingsley (1819-75) first came to Eversley as a curate, then was rector there from 1844 until he died. The many facets of his life — social reformer, educationalist, amateur scientist, hunting man, religious controversialist and poet – so typify the varied interests of English country clergymen that he seems in himself to represent the whole breed. His special brand of hearty Anglicanism was described in a phrase which has become part of the language: "muscular Christianity". So has another phrase he invented: "religion is the opium of the people." Meant as an approving metaphor for religion's benign effect, it was quoted by Marx with the opposite implication.

During his life Kingsley published many volumes of sermons, yet he suffered from an incapacitating stutter. Today he would be diagnosed as a manic depressive. Recent research has revealed another aspect of this complex man: he resolved his passionate sexual longings for his wife Fanny during their courtship by fantasizing religious humiliations for them to share, often naked, and sent her vivid drawings of these. The subsequent extravagance of his beloved Fanny was the cause of much of Kingsley's frenetic activity.

Of all that he did and wrote, Kingsley is best remembered for *The Water Babies*. This protest against the use of small boys as chimney sweeps was conceived at Eversley one spring morning in 1862, when Fanny observed that he had not yet written a book for their fourth child, baby Grenville. Kingsley returned half an hour later with its first and most inspired chapter.

A second of his books, *Alton Locke*, has found new popularity today as another early novel of social protest. It tells of the pathetic life of a tailor's apprentice, and is the literary counterpart of Kingsley's campaign for the improvement of a repulsively insanitary Thames-side slum.

Though he loved other parts of the country, it was to Eversley that he always returned. In this picturesque Surrey village, lying in green meadows on the river Blackwater within sound of the "blessed drums" of Aldershot, he cared for the red brick Georgian church, taught in the village school, defended tenants against landlords, and especially favoured his rougher parishioners who lived by poaching on the wild fringes of the parish.

However hard at work Kingsley might be in his rectory study, the sound of the hunt passing by would draw him out to follow. He kept a horse and regularly rode to hounds. He was a useful member of the hunt since he kept a register of Eversley foxes. ("Ain't they my parishioners?")

Kingsley's two least successful ventures were a period as Regius Professor of History at Cambridge, where he was also private tutor to the future Edward VII, and his attempt to confront Newman in print. Newman answered Kingsley's *What then does Dr Newman Mean?* with his *Apologia Pro Vita Sua*, which contemporaries agreed left Kingsley "cut to pieces and scattered about the theological battlefield".

Kingsley was so sure he would survive Fanny that when she fell ill with heart trouble he sat with her hour after hour in her icy bedroom planning every detail of her funeral. As a result he caught bronchitis and for a month the two of them were confined to beds at opposite ends of the rectory, communicating only by notes. Kingsley died, Fanny lived for another twenty years. Their graves lie side by side in Eversley churchyard.

Eversley rectory is today hardly changed. A cottage beside the village green, The Brewery, is where he lived as a curate.

William Kingsley
South Silvington, Yorkshire

William Kingsley (1815-1916), distressed by the attentions of village youths to his housemaids, fixed a notice to the back gate of his parsonage warning intruders that mantraps had been set in his grounds. He was describing his housemaids, he explained.

Though increasingly deaf, Kingsley loved music, founded a village orchestra, and in other ways he concerned himself with his parish, taking a particular interest in improving its drainage system. In addition he was a keen fisherman, carpenter and boat builder. One of the boats he built was so large that it could not be taken out of the shed in which he had built it.

For fifty years Kingsley was an examiner in mechanical drawing for the army. As such he was entitled to expenses and on one occasion he submitted: "Porter 6d". The authorities rejected this, saying that he was not entitled to claim for alcoholic drinks. When Kingsley explained that his claim was for a porter's tip, they replied that this should have been described as "Portage". The next time he needed to claim for the hire of a cab he submitted: "Cabbage 3s 6d".

Kingsley had been born in 1815, on the day of the battle of Waterloo, in which his father was taking part as an army surgeon. By 1915 he had held the living at South Silvington for fifty-five years and become known as "England's Oldest Rector". That year on his hundredth birthday, both the Archbishop of York and King George V wrote to send him their congratulations. He died the following year but remained sound in mind and a keen player of cribbage to the end.

William Kirby
Barham, Suffolk

In 1782 William Kirby (1759-1850) went to Barham to act as curate to the Rev N. Bacon who also held a neighbouring living. In 1797 Kirby became rector and stayed there till he died, a total of sixty-eight years. He had always been a keen botanist, but he turned to entomology when he accidentally found a beautiful insect. Bees became his passion and in 1802 he published his learned work, *Monographia Apium Angliae*. He collected 153 different specimens of wild bee species in his own parish.

Robert Eyres Landor
Birlingham, Worcestershire

Robert Landor (1781-1869) was vicar of Birlingham near Worcester for forty years from 1829. He suffered all his life from an ambition to emulate his more famous brother, the poet Walter Savage Landor, and from a lack of talent for doing so. He was encouraged when one of his anonymous poems was attributed to Lord Byron and for five years, before taking the living at Birlingham, he lived the life of a writer. However, after another poem, *The Impious Feast*, had been badly received, he abandoned his attempt.

Twelve years later he published three plays which had such poor reviews that he recovered all the copies he could find and burned them. At last in 1846 two historical novels set in classical times received the praise he hoped for, but thereafter he wrote nothing though he lived another twenty three years.

William Lee
Calverton, Nottinghamshire

William Lee (d. 1610), who was at Calverton, either as curate or incumbent, from 1589, here invented a stocking loom. In 1598 he presented Elizabeth I with a pair of silk stockings he had made on it. When the queen would not approve of his machine because it would discourage hand knitters, Lee went to live in France.

At Rouen, with the encouragement of the French king, he set up nine frames worked by nine English workmen, but he did not obtain the privileges he had been promised and died of disappointment in Paris. Seven of his workmen returned to England to become the founders of stocking manufacture here in this country.

John Lowes
Brandeston, Suffolk

John Lowes (1565-1645), vicar of Brandeston from 1595 for fifty years, was executed in 1645 for bewitching a ship which had sunk with all hands off Harwich. He was eighty years old. He confessed to the crime and admitted that "He had done many other hanous, wicked and accursed acts by the help of Six Impes . . . that frequented him daily." He was said to have made a covenant with the devil as a result of which he was marked with teats below his tongue and on the crown of his head. On the way to execution he read his own burial service.

John Lucy
Hampton Lucy, Warwickshire

In 1721-2 the Lucy family built on their estate at Hampton Lucy a classical and opulent rectory for the use of any member of the family who should wish for the living. John Lucy (1790-1874) was one such member; he was rector there for fifty-nine years.

Lucy's photograph shows a tall thin man, tightly wrapped in a frock coat, a high stock hiding his chin and a fur hat on his head. He was never an active priest, but respected and honoured by his parishioners as "a most perfect Gentleman of the Old School" who would "sweep off his hat with punctilious politeness to an old woman picking up sticks". He would dine from two till four, possessed a distinguished cellar, and planned his dinner parties like campaigns. But these sometimes failed, for when the Avon flooded, guests were unable to cross the ford to his rectory and had to turn back in view of his windows. In 1829 he solved this problem with an iron bridge, cast and erected at his own expense.

He rebuilt the church at Hampton Lucy to seat 400 people, and here he would give out fox hunting notices from the pulpit. Later in his incumbency he unfortunately allowed Sir Gilbert Scott to restyle the church's interior. He added a bedroom and breakfast room to the rectory, which opened directly on to its stableyard. The rectory still stands, though now named Hampton House.

At the age of eighty Lucy still came to meets, but on foot. Three years later in 1873 he fell ill with jaundice, but the amount of "Nourishment, Turtle Soup, Beef Tea, Consommé of Game and Meat, beside Champagne, Brandy and new milk he took every two hours . . . is almost indescribable – he sometimes drank a Bottle and a half of Champagne in twenty-four hours as well as a Bottle of Brandy in three days." His Alderney cow would be milked at one o'clock in the morning for a cup of fresh milk.

In the autumn of the same year he set out for London to acquire a new set of false teeth, although his doctors had told him the railway journey would kill him, and stayed there for six weeks, entertaining in his hotel and club. He died the next spring. His gravestone, beside a yew tree which he had planted in his churchyard, is still clearly inscribed.

Henry Lyte
Lower Brixham, Devon

Henry Lyte (1793-1847) is remembered as the author of the hymn *Abide with me; fast falls the eventide*, which has been described as "a very fine specimen of its kind, but the kind is all wrong". Its well-known tune by W.H. Monk was written in ten minutes. Lyte also wrote *Praise, my soul, the King of Heaven*. Much of his religious verse was composed while he was a curate at Lymington, Hampshire, though his volume of hymns was not published till 1834. By then he held the living of the new parish of Lower Brixham, where he went in 1826 and laboured for over twenty years.

Both Lyte and his son collected books – mainly poetry and theology. The year after Lyte's death the sale of his library took seventeen days. He is buried in the English Cemetery at Nice, where he died.

Thomas Robert Malthus
Albury, Surrey

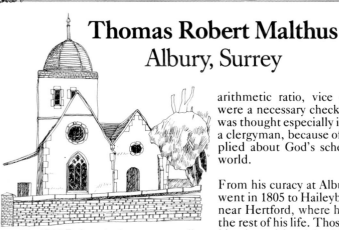

In 1798 Robert (as he was generally called) Malthus (1760-1834) published his notorious *Essay on Population* which caused such an outcry at the time, and added the word "Malthusian" to the English language. His thesis was that because population increased in a geometric ratio but subsistence only in an arithmetic ratio, vice and misery were a necessary check. This view was thought especially improper for a clergyman, because of what it implied about God's scheme for the world.

From his curacy at Albury Malthus went in 1805 to Haileybury College near Hertford, where he stayed for the rest of his life. Those who knew him there claimed that his personality bore little relationship to his theories. One friend for fifty years never saw him angry or ruffled. Another, Miss Martineau, reported that, although Malthus had a defective palate which made his speech hopelessly imperfect, he was the only friend she could hear without her ear trumpet.

Henry Edward Manning
Lavington, Sussex

Henry Manning (1808-92), later to become Cardinal Manning and Archbishop of Westminster, worked for seventeen years as a Church of England clergyman in the Sussex parish of Lavington. During part of that period he was also Archdeacon of Chichester.

As a boy at Harrow Manning had been such an outstanding captain of the cricket eleven that he was known as "The General". At Oxford he became an accomplished public speaker and was a brilliant student, gaining a first-class degree. He is said to have learned Italian while shaving. He grew to be disgusted by his father's idea that he should go into the Church and hoped instead for a political career. After his father's bankruptcy had made this ambition impossible he worked as a clerk in the Colonial Office, and only took Holy Orders when in 1833 he wanted to apply for a fellowship at Merton College, Oxford.

In the same year he obtained a curacy at Lavington, where six months later he succeeded to the living. Soon afterwards he married the previous rector's daughter. When she died after only four years, he sat inconsolable by her grave, writing his sermons. In retrospect he described the event as one of "God's special mercies" since it was "one of the chief agents in my conversion".

Manning was a conscientious parson, but his own feelings about his parish are unknown since he destroyed all his diary for the years before 1844 – as well as many later pages. He had been Newman's friend at Oxford and was drawn increasingly towards Roman Catholicism. In 1847-8 he visited Rome, where he had a long meeting with the Pope. His diary, otherwise extensive for this period, reported only "Audience today at the Vatican."

Manning's conversion to Roman Catholicism was finally provoked by the Gorham affair, in which the High Church Bishop Phillpotts of Exeter tried to exclude the Evangelical Mr Gorham from the living of Brampford Speke because of his views on Baptismal Regeneration. In Lytton Strachey's words, it became "all too clear [to Manning] that an Act of Parliament, passed by Jews, Roman Catholics, and Dissenters, was the ultimate authority which decided the momentous niceties of the Anglican faith."

In 1851, at a chapel off Buckingham Palace Road, London, Manning attended his last Church of England Communion service, accompanied by W.E. Gladstone, another Oxford friend. As the service began he told Gladstone that he could no longer make his Communion in the Church of England. "I rose up, and laying my hand on Mr Gladstone's shoulder, said 'Come'. It was the parting of ways. Mr Gladstone remained: and I went my way. Mr Gladstone still remains where I left him."

In 1865, fourteen years after his conversion, Manning succeeded Wiseman as Archbishop of Westminster. In 1875 he was created a cardinal. On his death bed, aged eight-five, he asked to be dressed in his full archbishop's vestments, and died wearing rochet and mozetta (surplice and cardinal's cope), his scarlet biretta on his head.

William Keble Martin
Coffinswell & Milber, Devon

Keble Martin (1877-1969), naturalist and illustrator, is famous for his *Concise British Flora in Colour*. Before the First World War he worked as a priest in Lancaster, then in the mining parish of Wath upon Dearne, Yorkshire. Though he had been a keen lepidopterist and botanist since his school days he was kept too busy with parish duties to pursue such interests until 1921 when he took the Devon living of Coffinswell. From here he would make expeditions all over the country in search of rare plants. Typically, after a Sunday of church services in July 1933, he took the midnight train to Perthshire, found two nice saxifrages on the clouded mountains the next morning, drew, coloured and replanted them the day after, then completed these and other drawings on the night train back to Devon.

In 1934 Martin became vicar of Torrington, where he was again too busy to make progress with his flower drawings. But in 1949, after a period at Milber, he retired "at the early age of seventy-two". He had become afraid that, because the lights on his autocycle went dim when climbing the hills around his parish, he might knock people down. He was then able to complete his drawings, which in total amounted to a hundred plates, showing in all 1,486 wild flower species.

Although the plates were exhibited by the Royal Horticultural Society in 1959, no publisher would risk the cost of colour reproduction, so an appeal was launched. Thirty-three plates were sent to the Duke of Edinburgh in the hope that he might help, but it was 1963 before George Rainbird agreed to publish the work.

By this time Martin's first wife had died and a Mrs Lewis was keeping house for him. After breakfast on October 26th 1964, at the age of eighty-seven, he suddenly proposed to Mrs Lewis, who refused him because she liked the name Lewis and would besides be financially ruined. Six weeks later Rainbird telephoned Martin to say that Prince Philip had agreed to write a foreword to *Concise British Flora*. "In the joy and excitement of the moment Mrs Lewis forgot her reserve and threw her arms around me." They were married next January.

In 1967 Martin's flower illustrations were used for a special issue of 4d postage stamps.

John Mason
Water Stratford, Buckinghamshire

John Mason (*c.* 1645-94) proclaimed that the Second Coming of the Messiah would occur in his own parish of Water Stratford on Whit Sunday 1694. In preparation for this day great crowds gathered, filling every house and outhouse in the village. Many had sold all their possessions and practised community of goods, "even to a point outraging decency". An eyewitness who visited the rectory found a great congregation "walking round the hall in a ring, making a prodigious noise and all of them crying out 'Glory! Glory!

Glory!' and all in a sweat, and looking as if they were mad."

At the height of the excitement, after addressing the crowd from his chamber window, Mason was struck dumb with a quinsy from which he soon died. When his followers began to claim that they had seen him risen from the dead on a piece of holy ground near the rectory, Mason's successor, Mr Rushworth, had him dug up to show them his corpse. Despite this they continued to meet in a house in the parish where, sixteen years later, the same eyewitness saw them still processing in a ring and making the same noise.

John Mavor
Forest Hill, Oxfordshire

John Mavor (1786-1853), son of William Mavor, the rector of Bladon with Woodstock, fell dramatic victim to the Victorian ambition for a prestigious parsonage. His troubles started at Lincoln, his Oxford college, where, when he refused the position of Greek lecturer, the college Rector wrote that "so much ignorance and irreverence in a fellow I never before encountered." Perhaps he referred to Mavor's betting habits. Mavor's name appears frequently in the common room betting book: "What was the family name of the Athlones? Mavor was right. How many shares had Pierce Walsh in the Oxford canal? Mavor knew the answer. Would Mavor get £20 for his pony? Mavor did."

Nevertheless, in 1823 the college offered Mavor the "Perpetual Curacy" of the little village of Forest Hill just to the east of Oxford. The income was only £30 a year, but to augment this he was also given the Essex living of Hadleigh. Mavor excused himself for never living at Hadleigh by saying that it was "situated in an aguish and very unhealthy part of the Essex coast". Instead, he began to build at Forest Hill "one of the most convenient and complete places of residence in the Diocese". It left him in serious debt.

Two years after it was finished he was forced to sell his books and some furniture. After another two years his own lawyer, to whom he owed less than £10, had him imprisoned for eight months.

He was released, but in 1843 an Oxford tradesman, after seizing and selling the few articles of furniture Mavor had acquired, again caused him to be put in prison. He continued, however, to believe that Lincoln College owed him a living and to write letters of appeal to the Bishop of Lincoln. These were ineffectual and in 1853 he died, still in the debtors' prison.

William Fordyce Mavor
Bladon with Woodstock, Oxfordshire

William Mavor (1758-1837), scholar and author, wrote a spelling book which went into many editions and which was apparently translated into a number of languages, including Burmese. A school inspector referred to it as "Mavor's Exploded Spelling Book". It was still in use as the chief secular textbook in a workhouse in 1847, forty-five years after its publication.

He also devised a system of shorthand, and published, among many other works, an appendix to the Eton Latin grammar, *The Lady's and Gentleman's Botanical Pocket Book*, a poem and guide to the Palace of Blenheim, and a world history of voyages, travels and discoveries in twenty-five volumes.

He is buried at Woodstock, where his tombstone, near the church door, carries a long admiring inscription, saying among other things that he was "ten times Mayor of this borough".

Jack William Mitchell
Cotleigh, Devon

Jack Mitchell (1805-69) was rector of Cotleigh near Honiton from 1827 for thirty-four years. His father, grandfather and great-grandfather had been rectors there before him. He was a sporting parson who hunted, fished and shot. He kept his own pack of badger hounds with which he would hunt badgers in Court Wood on early summer evenings.

For shooting he used a Joe Manton muzzle loader and would often bring down birds with left and right barrels. Of shooting pheasants he said: "When a bird rises, take out your snuff-box, have a good pinch of snuff, then shoot the bird."

John Mitford
Benhall, Suffolk

John Mitford (1781-1859) was installed at Benhall near Saxmundham in 1810 and remained vicar there for the next forty-nine years. Few of his neighbours, however, sought his company except under protest. His wife left him and his only son would not speak to him. He "took under his wing" a twelve-year-old village girl called Eliza, and he was rumoured to have dealings with Satan. After his death he was remembered in the village as the wicked old parson who haunted Mitford Lane.

Others were charmed by Mitford and by his extensive library and garden of exotic trees. Charles Lamb called him "a pleasant layman spoiled" and wrote to a friend, "Your description of Mr Mitford's place makes me long for a pippin, some caraways and a cup of sack in his orchard when the sweets of night come in."

Mitford preferred his London lodgings in Sloane Street where, for seventeen years from 1834, he edited the *Gentleman's Magazine*. During this time his own monthly contributions never failed to appear. His friend, Mrs Houston, found that his "brilliancy of conversation was entirely unmarred by any desire to shine". He was her invariably accurate source of information on any subject and often conveyed this to her in doggerel verse. But the death-bed terrors of this "ripe scholar and kindly friend" were painful in the extreme, because of his fear of the approaching punishment for his misdeeds.

Giles Moore
Horsted Keynes, Sussex

Giles Moore (*c.* 1617-79), rector of Horsted Keynes for twenty-four years till his death in 1679, kept a diary which largely consisted of a record of the cost of living. From it his style of dress can be pictured: two pairs of gloves "faced with my own fringe" (2s 3d and 1s 4d); a silk levitical girdle (10s); two worsted canonical girdles (5s); a waistcoat of "Devonshire red blazes"(7s 4d); a pair of silk stockings (£1 1s); "silken tops" (6s 6d); a pair of black worsted stockings (5s); "a shaggy demicastor hat of fashion" (16s 6d).

Occasionally Moore engaged in barter:

"I sent to Mr Hely a ribspare and hoggs puddings for which hee returned me a box of pills and sermons."

"I sent Mistresse Michelborne a galon of rose water and 1 quart of damasks, shee sending me back by the messenger 3 dozen pigeons."

When the son of a fellow rector wanted to marry his daughter Moore wrote with caution: "I do not so little value you, nor your son, but that if the young man could fancy her for a wyfe this advowson and that well stocked . . . together also with library when I leave this world, I should not . . . judge her amisse bestowed." The marriage did not take place.

Moore was keenly interested in his brother's will and possible legacies; he describes in detail in his diary the progress of the brother's illness. When suffering from a high fever the brother "came forth speedily and leaped into a well which was ten feete deep in water, out of which he was quickly taken and put into a warme bed". He died the next week and Moore costs his funeral.

William Morgan
Llanrhaiadr ym Mochant, Denbighshire

William Morgan (1540-1604), who held the living of the remote parish of Llanrhaiadr, here produced the first translation of the Bible into Welsh. Parishioners brought complaints that he was not qualified for the task to his bishop, who in turn sent him on to Archbishop Whitgift at Lambeth; but Whitgift was so impressed by Morgan's Greek and Hebrew scholarship that he made him his chaplain and undertook the full cost of the work.

Morgan was made Bishop of St Asaph's in 1595. He is buried in the choir of the cathedral. Three hundred years later in 1888 a memorial was erected to him in the cathedral precincts.

Henry Moule
Fordington, Dorset

Henry Moule (1801-80) was vicar of Fordington for fifty-one years from 1829. He was so dismayed here by the cholera epidemics which were common in the countryside at this time that he devised and, in 1860, patented a lavatory which "flushed" with dry earth. He had previously published (at the price of 1s) *Four Letters to Prince Albert on the Dwellings and Conditions of the Working Classes and Poor of Fordington*.

Thomas Mozley
Cholderton, Wiltshire

Thomas Mozley (1806-93), the journalist who married Cardinal Newman's sister Harriet, got into financial difficulties when he tried to build an excessively large church for his remote parish of Cholderton on Salisbury Plain. He made it big so that it would fit under a second-hand oak roof he had discovered lying on a quay at Ipswich. He imported to Cholderton both the roof and a team of Suffolk workmen, and spent £5,000 of his own money on the project, but the church remained unfinished until 1850, three years after Mozley had left the parish.

During his time at Cholderton Mozley had become editor of the *British Critic*, the chief organ of the Tractarian Movement. Sometimes he would travel to London on editorial business, arriving at 5.30 in the morning and walking up and down Fleet Street until the printers opened at seven. More often he would send his material by coach. "Several coaches passed through my parish, one of them about an hour or two after midnight, changing horses a mile off. Night after night I took my parcel to the changing house, and had sometimes to wait a long time. My practised ears became quick and sensitive. I could always hear the coach emerging out of a depression and passing Stonehenge, seven miles off; then rattling past Vespasian's Camp into Amesbury; and after changing horses, toiling up Beacon Hill, down which it then came at a hand gallop."

In 1844, soon after he had given up his editorship, Mozley began to write leading articles for *The Times*; this he continued to do almost daily for many years. In 1868 he took the Devon living of Plymtree where, apart from a five-month spell as *The Times* correspondent in Rome, he remained for the rest of his life. He was described as "an active thinker in a desultory sort of way", and his *Reminiscences* are full of amusing gossip about his contemporaries.

George Murray
Hurston, Kent

Lord George Murray (1761-1803), who held the living of Hurston at the time of the French Revolutionary wars, applied his skills to "the telegraph", a kind of semaphore, and was made manager of the telegraph at various English ports as well as on Wimbledon Common. Later he became director of the telegraph at the Admiralty in London.

In 1798 he recruited troops from his Kent parish to oppose a French invasion, but he was rebuked for such zeal by the bishops in conference at Lambeth. In 1801 Lord George was made Bishop of St David's but he died two years later of a chill which he caught while waiting for his carriage outside the House of Lords.

William Nelson
Brandon Parva, Norfolk

Two scandals, neither of them true, are connected with William Nelson (1757-1835), the eldest brother of Horatio, Viscount Nelson. The first accused him, as a naval chaplain in the West Indies, of drawing pay without performing his duties. His brother, the ship's captain, was said to have known of this irregularity, but the pay book of the *Boreas* proves that he in fact drew no pay. The second scandal suggested that he concealed the last codicil of Horatio's will, which was in favour of Lady Hamilton, until he had received the grant which he hoped the government would make him as a reward for his brother's services. In fact the government officers had seen the complete will from the start and knew of the legacy.

Nelson's greater interest lies in the many letters that his brother wrote to him. William Nelson and his wife often received Horatio as their guest at Brandon Parva and they were on intimate terms with Lady Hamilton.

He was a large, heavy, boisterous man, with a loud voice, "exceedingly and impatiently deaf". After his brother's death at Trafalgar he inherited the title. He also received a pension of £5,000 a year and a grant of £90,000 with which he bought Stanlynch Park near Downton in Wiltshire.

John Newton
Olney, Buckinghamshire

John Newton (1725-1807), later to become the devout Methodist and hymn writer of Olney, had one of the most remarkable early lives of any Anglican clergyman. At nineteen he was press-ganged into H.M.S. *Harwich* and promoted to midshipman before he deserted ship. Recaptured and flogged, he was again made a seaman.

Off Madeira he asked to be transferred to a slaver which took him to the West Indies. "From this time," he wrote, "I was exceedingly vile indeed. I not only sinned with a high hand myself, but made it my study to tempt and seduce others upon every occasion." Presently he worked for a slave trader whose black mistress made him her own slave. His only comfort was solving Euclidean geometric problems in the sand. Escaping from this master, he then worked for a better one who gave Newton a share in his slave factory.

In 1748 on his way home, while steering the ship in a storm, Newton had a religious experience which transformed his life. Ever afterwards he celebrated its anniversary. However, he made several more slaving voyages, conducting daily prayers on deck.

Newton took Holy Orders only when ill health prevented him from slaving, and was not appointed curate in charge of Olney until he was almost forty. Here he became the friend of the poet William Cowper; and he bears some responsibility for inducing the states of religious mania from which Cowper suffered. For over a year Cowper lived with Newton at the vicarage, and together the two would go parish visiting. Together they wrote the *Olney Hymns*, of which were 68 were by Cowper and 280 by Newton.

Newton's Evangelical activities at Olney took the form of incessant preaching, both in the village and in the houses and cottages of the neighbourhood, and of prayer meetings which friends and neighbouring dissenting ministers attended. But not all his parishioners supported him and when, on November 5th 1779, he tried to check some dangerous orgies, there were such disturbances that he had to pay money to protect his house from attack. Soon afterwards he left Olney, disillusioned by the results of his work there. In London he continued to preach for over twenty-five years; his final sermon, given in 1806, during which he forgot his subject, was for the sufferers from the battle of Trafalgar.

Conrad le Despenser Roden Noel
Thaxted, Essex

Conrad Noel (1869-1942), grandson of the first Earl of Gainsborough and vicar of Thaxted from 1910 until he died, was notorious for his left-wing views. He hoisted the red flag in the parish and preached Christian socialism. Towards the end of the First World War he launched his Christian Crusade, with the explicit aim of creating a socialist economic system. At a meeting near Covent Garden he welcomed the Russian Revolution. Early in life he had listed his recreations as "long distance running, swimming, chess, debating and discussion". Later he reduced them to "political and theological controversy".

At Thaxted – according to Jack Putterill who was his curate and successor – Noel made the "wonderful Gothic church" into "a colourful dream". Noel's wife, Miriam, designed the curtains. Here in the church, dressed in the full rig of a mediaeval priest, he conducted services which re-introduced the dramatic ritual of the middle ages, with appropriate ceremonial and plainsong. This last was sung without organ accompaniment, "freely and quickly as it should be". Confessions were heard and weddings held in the church porch, as in mediaeval times. The wedding cake and a silver goblet of wine were blessed and then carried in procession round the church.

Francis North
Old Alresford, Hampshire

Francis North (d. 1861), Earl of Guildford, a notorious pluralist, was given the three livings of Old Alresford, New Alresford and Medstead by his father, Bishop Brownlow North of Winchester; these brought in an annual income of £1,410. He also held St Mary's, the best living in Southampton, which was worth £2,000 a year and was a prebendary of Winchester; this gave him another £1,000 annually.

In 1808 North's father made him Master of the mediaeval almshouses near Winchester known as the Hospital of St Cross. During the next forty-one years one estimate suggests that North profited from this position by £305,700. He

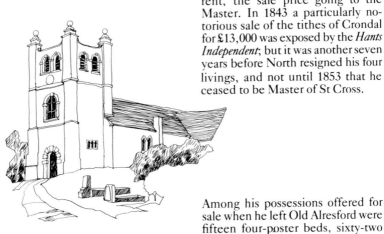

rent, the sale price going to the Master. In 1843 a particularly notorious sale of the tithes of Crondal for £13,000 was exposed by the *Hants Independent*; but it was another seven years before North resigned his four livings, and not until 1853 that he ceased to be Master of St Cross.

obtained this vast sum by selling the leases of the hospital's properties for many years ahead, the hospital itself receiving only a tiny annual

Among his possessions offered for sale when he left Old Alresford were fifteen four-poster beds, sixty-two dozen bottles of port, claret, madeira, champagne, hock and hermitage wines, and two butts of fine ale.

Alexander Nowell
Much Hadham, Hertfordshire

Alexander Nowell (*c.* 1517-1602), rector of Much Hadham from 1562 for twenty-seven years, invented bottled beer. This he devised to take with him when he went fishing in the river Ash, a hobby which occupied much of his time. After leaving Much Hadham he became Principal of his old Oxford college, Brasenose.

Titus Oates
Bobbing, Kent

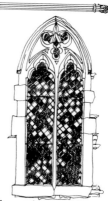

Titus Oates (1649-1705), the notorious perjurer, first held the living of Bobbing in Kent; here he met his fellow plotter, the Rev Israel Tonge. He moved next to be his father's curate at Hastings, where he was imprisoned for collaborating with his father in fabricating a "very disgraceful" charge against a local schoolmaster.

Escaping from Dover Castle, Oates was briefly a naval chaplain, and then chaplain at Arundel Castle before returning to London where he again met Tonge and where they planned their supremely profitable "disclosures". To prepare for these Oates studied at Catholic seminaries in Valladolid and St Omer (he was expelled from both) in order to worm his way into Roman Catholic circles, before bringing his accusations to Sir Edmund Berry Godfrey in 1679.

The accusations included three separate Catholic plots to murder King Charles II (by shooting, knifing and poisoning). Many leading Catholics were arrested and convicted, largely on Oate's invented evidence. Eventually thirty-five were executed or died in prison. For four years Oates was successful with his perjuries, ultimately walking about London dressed as a bishop and naming virtually anyone he chose as subversive. He claimed not only a salary, but also huge expenses from the House of Commons for his "loyal" work. A first bill was for £678 12s 6d.

When James II with his Catholic sympathies succeeded to the throne in 1685 Oates was convicted of perjury and sentenced to be whipped from Aldgate to Newgate, then from Newgate to Tyburn, to be imprisoned for life and to stand annually in the pillory. Released in 1688 after James II had been displaced by William III, Oates fathered a son by a bedmaker in the King's Bench Prison before taking a modestly prosperous wife, whose fortune he soon exhausted. Thereafter he was often poor despite an eventual treasury grant and pension. Briefly he became a Baptist but was expelled when he was discovered plotting to extract a legacy from a rich devotee.

Sydney Godolphin Osborne
Durweston, Dorset

After nine years at Stoke Poges, Sydney Osborne (1808-89) became rector of Durweston on the Dorset downs. Here he remained from 1841 to 1875, and here he began the series of letters to *The Times* for which he is remembered. Always signed S.G.O., these continued for the next forty-four years, earning him a reputation as a militant philanthropist. Few causes of the time – from Free Trade and the Irish problem, to sanitation, women's rights, cattle plague and cholera – escaped his attention. In 1855 during the Crimean War he made a private visit to Florence Nightingale's hospital at Scutari and published a pamphlet on his findings.

Married to one of the Grenville sisters, Emily, Osborne became Charles Kingsley's brother-in-law when Kingsley married another sister, Fanny. It was Osborne's introduction of Kingsley to the appalling living conditions of Dorset labourers that awoke Kingsley's social conscience. But despite their work for the same causes, Kingsley was critical of Osborne, writing that he could not be relied on for support when "the dirt is not of his own finding".

When describing his own domestic plans, Kingsley gives a picture of the Osbornes' living style in their large rectory with its avenue of clipped yews. In imitation of the Osbornes, Kingsley planned to have "a man to groom and garden and wait at table when there is company (£25), a cook (£25) who must do some housemaid's work, a maid (£25) to look after you, our bedroom, and to wait on us when we are alone . . . We shall be richer than the Osbornes for I shall keep only one horse."

Osborne retired for Durweston to Lewes, Sussex, where his final series of letters to *The Times* concerned the notorious Whitechapel murders.

Joseph Paisley
Springfield, Dumfriesshire

Joseph Paisley, though never ordained, was one of the most notorious of those who usurped the marrying functions of English parsons by performing weddings beyond the Scottish border. Paisley operated first at Gretna, and then, from 1791 to 1814, at the nearby village of Springfield.

A tall, heavily built man, Paisley was called the "Blacksmith". He had a stentorian voice and such strength that he could bend straight a horseshoe with his hands. In various forms of toddy and in neat drams he would drink a pint of whisky a day. Late in life he grew enormous until he weighed twenty-five stone.

His customers were frequently involved in chases over the nine miles between Carlisle and Gretna when "the beautiful daughters of England . . . with whip and spur and shout, and wild halloo" would gallop towards the border, pursued by a guardian, jilted lover or angry father "urging on postboys who also whipped and spurred and hallooed, but took care never to overtake the fugitives until too late".

This highly profitable trade began after 1753, when the traditional marrying places for runaway couples around Ludgate Hill and in the Fleet Prison in London were closed. By the 1850s it is estimated that a thousand marriages a year were being performed along the Scottish border. But in 1857 a new law compelled both parties to live in Scotland for six weeks before the wedding day.

William Douglas Parish
Selmeston, Sussex

William Parish (1833-1904), vicar of Selmeston and of neighbouring Alciston for forty-one years from 1863, is best known for his *Dictionary of the Sussex Language.*

Selmeston (at that time pronounced "Simpson") is a tiny village lying on the northern edge of the South Downs. Here Parish collected the material for his original work in rustic scholarship by continuous close contact with his parishioners. He was no rustic himself but the son of the diplomat Sir Woodbine Parish, and educated at Charterhouse and Trinity College, Oxford. In middle age his portrait shows a broad-faced, side-whiskered man with a watch chain – more like a squire than a priest.

The dictionary, first published in 1875 and reprinted in expanded form in 1957, contains many entertaining examples of Sussex usage, for example:
Thick-of-hearing . . .

Old woman, old woman, will you go a shearing?
Speak a little louder, sir, I'm rather thick of hearing.
Old woman, old woman, shall I kiss you very sweetly?
I thank you very kindly, sir, I hear you quite completely.
          Old Sussex Rhyme.

Parish's aim in compiling his dictionary was to preserve British, Roman, Saxon and Norman "words in everyday use among labouring people, who retain among them many of the oldest forms of words which . . . have long ago become obsolete among their superiors."

Among his other works are *The Telegraphist's Easy Guide*, written to teach the boys of Selmeston the Morse code, and *School Attendance without Compulsion*, a booklet suggesting that truancy could be prevented by returning school payments to the parents of regular attenders.

Parish's tombstone can be found in his own churchyard. Selmeston church itself is his other memorial; he supervised its rebuilding in 1867, personally marking the stones for re-setting, but fortunately leaving intact its unusual fourteenth-century timber pillars and arcade.

Samuel Parr
Hatton, Warwickshire

Samuel Parr (1747-1825), schoolmaster at Stanmore, then "Perpetual Curate" at Hatton, had in his time a considerable literary reputation which has not survived. Sydney Smith wrote in 1800 that Parr seemed to believe eloquence consisted of "a studious arrangement of sonorous, exotic, and sesquipedal words", and after Parr's death that "He would have been a more considerable man if he had been more knocked about among his equals. He lived with country gentlemen and clergymen, who flattered and feared him."

At Stanmore Parr married a wife who neither flattered nor feared him but "took pleasure in exposing his foibles and peculiarities before company". He had, she said, been "born in a whirlwind and bred a tyrant".

In 1820 Parr became for a year chaplain to George IV's unfortunate Queen Caroline. He died five years later of a cold caught at a parishioner's funeral.

William Paul
Orton on the Hill, Leicestershire

As soon as he heard of the rising of 1715, William Paul (1679-1716) set out from his parish of Orton to join the Jacobite forces in Lancashire, reaching them at Preston.

After the defeat of the rebellion Paul came to London where he was recognized by Tom Byrd, a magistrate from Claybrooke near Orton, arrested, charged with treason and condemned to death.

In an attempt to save his life Paul pleaded guilty and claimed now to abhor the rebellion, but when this tactic failed he again changed his views. In July 1716 he appeared at Tyburn in the canonical dress of the Church of England, declared that he was now a true son of the Church and asked pardon for pleading guilty. He was hanged, drawn and quartered. "I wish", he said, "that I had enough quarters to send to every parish in the kingdom, to testify that a clergyman of the Church of England was martyred for being loyal to the King."

Because of his arrest of Paul, Tom Byrd became known in Orton as "Kill Parson" and he soon afterwards moved from the district.

Octavius Pickard-Cambridge
Bloxworth, Dorset

Octavius Pickard-Cambridge (1828-1917), rector of Bloxworth near Poole from 1867 for the next fifty years, has been called the "Father of British Spiders". His first paper on spiders appeared in *The Zoologist* in 1859. Twenty-one years later he had published eighty. His collection of carefully preserved specimens (in contrast to those of others whom he described as "the goodness gracious scientists") is now in the British Museum. His masterwork, *Spiders of Dorset*, in fact covers the whole country. The initials O.P-C. after the scientific names of 115 spider species credit him with first describing them. He was a friend

of Darwin and corresponded with him on many subjects including the sex life of the spider.

Pickard-Cambridge's father had been rector of Bloxworth before him, as well as squire, and though Octavius was the fifth son of fifteen brothers and sisters, he too virtually assumed the role of "squarson", since his elder brothers mostly left Bloxworth House empty. At the rectory his scientific work was carried out in his "Den". Here he corresponded with arachnidists all over the world, receiving and examining their reports and specimens. Later his well-trained sons also reported to him.

Behind the rectory stood an abandoned malt house with two vats. These he would fill with hot water every Saturday evening for the boys and girls of his Sunday school to bath in. He had still more mediaeval

dealings with his employees, part-paying them with his own home-made cheese. When, in protest, these cheeses were used to prop open the gates of the village street, he had them collected and brought home for further use.

Pickard-Cambridge also held the nearby living of the tiny hamlet of Winterbourne Tomson to which he would go on foot to hold services, often in an empty church. When the church there was closed in 1890 he calculated that in reaching it each Sunday he had walked in total 7,000 miles.

Though Hardy did not use Bloxworth as the model for Bathsheba Everdine's house in *Far from the Madding Crowd*, it was used in Schlesinger's film, as was Bloxworth churchyard where Sergeant Troy and Fanny Robin were buried.

Lionel Playters
Uggeshall, Suffolk

In 1644 Lionel Playters (*c.* 1606-79), rector of Uggeshall, was one of the Royalist parsons ejected from his living by the Earl of Manchester's Committee for Scandalous Ministers.

Among other things he was accused of spending the day of August 31st 1642 "drinking with a papist and armorer, since gone to royal army", and of having said that he hoped to sell his hemp well "for if theis tymes hold many would need hanging", and that he had ten stone of hemp he would bestow freely to hang up the Roundheads. Furthermore, when salt was spilled he said, "save the salt for salt will be deare . . . the

Roundheads must be salted." But the prime cause of his ejection, according to John Walker, was "his Eating Custard after a scandalous manner"; he apparently added sack to it and ate it with great greediness.

Players survived, and again held his living after the Restoration from 1660 until he died.

Thomas Porter
East Hoathly, Sussex

We know of Thomas Porter 1719-95), vicar of East Hoathly from 1752 until his death, through the diary of Thomas Turner, who was Porter's churchwarden and the village grocer. In February and March 1757 the village was overtaken by an orgy of drinking and merry-making, in which Porter played a full part. On one evening, "After supper our behaviour was far from that of serious, harmless mirth; it was downright obstreperous, mixed with a great deal of folly and stupidity. Our diversion was dancing or jumping about, without a violin or any musick, singing of foolish healths, and drinking all the time as fast as it could be well poured down; and the parson of the parish was one among the mixed multitude."

At six the next morning, less than an hour after Mrs Turner had got to bed, the vicar's wife woke her, pretending to want some cream of tartar, then insisted she come downstairs where "she found Mr Porter, Mr Fuller and his wife, with a lighted candle, and part of a bottle of wine and a glass. The next thing", Turner continues, "was to have me down stairs, which being apprized of, I fastened my door. Up stairs they came, and threatened to break it open; so I ordered the boys to open it, when they poured into my room; and, as modesty forbid me to get out of bed, so I refrained; but their immodesty permitted them to draw me out of bed, as the common phrase is, topsy-turvey; but, however, at the intercession of Mr Porter, they permitted me to put on my ———, and, instead of my upper clothes, they gave me time to put on my wife's petticoats; and in this manner they made me dance, without shoes and stockings, until they had emptied the bottle of wine, and also a bottle of my beer . . . About three o'clock in the afternoon, they found their way to their respective homes, beginning to be a little serious."

At a supper party a few days later "We continued drinking like horses, as the vulgar phrase is, and singing till many of us were very drunk, and then we went to dancing and pulling wigs, caps, and hats; and thus we continued in this frantic manner behaving more like mad people than they that profess the name of Christians." The following night they behaved similarly at the vicar's house. Next day Turner wrote "At home all day. Very piteous." And a week later "Now I hope all revelling for this season is over."

Turner found the vicar's wife a person of changeable moods. On one occasion she "treated me with as much imperious and scornful usage as if she had been what I think she is, more of a Turk and Infidel, than a Christian, and I an abject slave." But later when he told her a gown she had ordered would be late, she "received me with all the affability, courtesy, and good humour imaginable. Oh! what a pleasure would it be to serve them was they always in such a temper."

Porter and his wife are commemorated by a memorial behind the rector's stall in East Hoathly church, which also records that they had five daughters who died in infancy.

Francis Potter
Kilmington, Wiltshire

Francis Potter (1594-1678) remained a commoner of Trinity College, Oxford for many years, but when his father died in 1628 he succeeded to the living of Kilmington, a development which John Aubrey regretted. "'Twas pitty that such a delicate inventive Witt should be staked to a private preferment in an obscure corner where he wanted ingeniose conversations, from whence men rarely emerge to higher preferment, but contract a mosse on them like an old pale in an orchard . . ." Here Potter remained, however, escaping sequestration during the Civil War.

A man of numerous skills, Potter had an inventive mind. Most of his devices were mechanical, and he built among other things quadrants with a graduated compass of his own design. He also drew and painted for his own enjoyment.

His blood transfusion theory of 1640 was one of the earliest. He and Aubrey tried to confirm it experimentally using a hen, but the creature was "too little" and their tools "not good"; Aubrey therefore sent him a surgeon's lancet, but to what effect he does not say. Aubrey also sent Potter's results to the Royal Society, of which Potter, in 1663, became one of the earliest fellows.

Some of Potter's other speculations were more fantastic, in particular

that which made 25 the "appropinque" square root of 666 and the basis for an elaborate theory about the Number of the Beast in the Book of Revelation. Nevertheless his book, *Interpretation of the Number 666*, was described by a contemporary as "a wonderful discovery, the happiest that ever yet came into the world", and Pepys called it "mighty ingenious".

Always sickly, Potter seemed to Aubrey "the most like a Monk, or one of the Pastours of old time, that ever I saw one." Potter kept his house as undecked as a monk's cell. In old age, however, he became blind and let his beard remain uncut. Asked why he did not invite a relative

to look after him, he replied that he had tried some of them but preferred servants since they did not begrudge what he spent and were kinder to him. He is buried in the chancel of Kilmington church.

John Cyril Putterill
Thaxted, Essex

Jack Putterill (1892-1980) began his working life in the Midland Bank. On a walking tour in 1914 he came to Thaxted, fell under the influence of its radical vicar, Conrad Noel, and adopted his High Church and socialist opinions. Later Putterill married Noel's daughter, Barbara. While still at the bank he took Holy Orders, and first went as a curate to Coleford in Gloucestershire and then to the mining town of Abertillery. Here, at a parish church council meeting, one of the churchwardens proposed "That the vicar should forbid the curate any further preaching and the calling of the miners slaves." The vicar advised Putterill to "Wrap it up a bit more, man."

In 1925 Putterill returned to Thaxted as Noel's curate. Here he gathered a band – at one time twenty-strong – of assorted instrumentalists to augment the mediaeval plainsong of the church services. Traditional music and dancing, in particular Morris dancing, were his great interests. He joined the Thaxted Morris team and claimed to dance and sing a jig every morning in the bathroom. Astronomy was his other interest. He found an old six-foot long telescope in a parishioner's shed, mounted it in his garden on an old car engine for stability, and photographed the heavens.

In the mid-1930s when the hunger marchers passed through Saffron Walden, Putterill addressed a meeting at the fountain. He was charged

with obstruction and fined five shillings.

For five years Putterill was vicar of Plaistow in the East End of London, then in 1942 returned to Thaxted to succeed Noel as vicar. Here he continued Noel's work. In 1946 he became an Essex county councillor for the Labour Party. When he retired to Saffron Walden at the age of eighty-one his farewell gift from the Thaxted Morris team was the transfer and re-erection of his observatory in his new garden.

James Ramsay
Teston and Nettlestead, Kent

James Ramsay (1733-89) was one of the earliest anti-slavery campaigners. He had his first experience of the slave trade when, as a naval surgeon, he was called to the assistance of a slaver struck by the plague. A broken thigh, which lamed him for life, caused him to leave the navy and take Holy Orders. He then held several livings in the West Indies where he gave medical help as well as religious instruction to the slaves, activities which aroused such anger among slave owners that he left those parts.

After further adventures, once more as a naval chaplain, Ramsay returned to England in 1781 and obtained the living of Teston in Kent. Three years later he published *An Essay on the Treatment and Conversion of African Slaves in the British Sugar Colonies*, one of the most important events in the early history of the anti-slavery movement. He was consulted by Wilberforce, and by Pitt. But bitter attacks on him in Parliament upset his health, and he died at the age of fifty-five. He is buried at Teston where a tablet on the church wall commemorates him.

Jeremiah Ravens
Great Blakenham, Suffolk

Jeremiah Ravens (b. 1600) was rector of Great Blakenham from 1631 until 1644, when he was ejected by the Earl of Manchester's Committee for Scandalous Ministers. Among other views hateful to the Parliamentarians, he had preached that holy days should be observed before Sundays, and that those not coming to the rails for sacrament would be damned.

He was said to be often drunk, to have kept "a whore one Coles wife", and to have "hunge his wife upp by the heeles and tyed [her] to the bedposts and whipped her". A crucifix and several popish pictures found in his house suggest that he was a secret Roman Catholic.

Leigh Richmond
Turvey, Bedfordshire

L eigh Richmond (1772-1827), author and earnest Evangelical, was a curate at Bradbury in the Isle of Wight for eight years. Here he collected material for his three tales of village life, originally published in the *Christian Guardian*. The first of these, *The Dairyman's Daughter*, was translated into French, Italian, German, Danish and Swedish, and sold two million copies in English during his lifetime.

When Richmond moved to Turvey in Bedfordshire he became a well known preacher, in demand all over the country. While on preaching tours he wrote letters to his children enquiring about the states of their souls. He brought them up on strict Evangelical principles: "No games of chance, fishing, field sports, dancing, theatre-going, novels, oratorios, intimacy with the servants or unsuitable acquaintances."

John Rous
Santon Downham, Suffolk

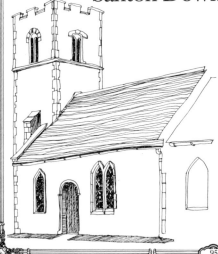

J ohn Rous (1584-1644), who held the living of the small village of Santon Downham from 1623 till he died, kept a diary in which he included satirical verses and sayings of his time.

Rous lived in the parsonage of the next-door parish of Weeting where, over two hundred years later in 1856, the Rev Vyvyan Luke, who then held the living, believed "that the very room in which I am now penning these lines, was the one in which a portion of the diary was written". A few years before, Luke had dug up an old brick floor in the house and "underneath I came to a thick bed of clay, embedded in which were bones of almost every description of animal used for food; beef, mutton, pork, rabbits, fowls, etc, speaking most forcibly of the habits of olden time."

Martin Joseph Routh
Tilehurst, Berkshire

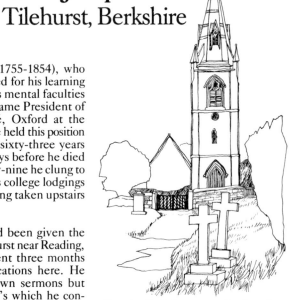

Martin Routh (1755-1854), who was renowned for his learning and retained all his mental faculties to a great age, became President of Magdalen College, Oxford at the age of thirty-six. He held this position for the remaining sixty-three years of his life. Two days before he died at the age of ninety-nine he clung to the banisters in his college lodgings to stop himself being taken upstairs to bed.

Meanwhile he had been given the rich living of Tilehurst near Reading, and he always spent three months of the Oxford vacations here. He never wrote his own sermons but delivered Towson's which he considered the best, so why should he do more than shorten them to fifteen minutes?

Routh died intestate, having forgotten to sign his will; he is buried in Magdalen chapel.

Daniel Rowlands
Llangeitho, Cardiganshire

Daniel Rowlands (1713-90) was one of those principally responsible for the rise of Methodism in Wales. In 1733, when his father died and his brother John obtained the living at Llangeitho, Daniel became his brother's curate. Here he preached – almost always in Welsh – to such effect that his hearers "trembled and cried out for mercy". Families would travel fifty or sixty miles to hear him. In the churchyard they would lie overnight so thickly packed that it was difficult to pass without treading on them. On Sundays he would give Communion to between 1,500 and 2,500 people.

From Llangeitho Rowlands travelled to preach in other parishes, where he was resented by the incumbents and disliked for his extremism. Once an assassin attempted to shoot him and pulled the trigger of his pistol, but it failed to fire. On another occasion a charge of powder was found below his preaching place.

In 1760 Daniel's brother died and he might have expected to succeed to the living of Llangeitho; but the Bishop of St David's gave it instead to Daniel's son, also named John. Nevertheless Daniel stayed at Llangeitho as his son's curate until, three years later, the bishop withdrew his licence to preach. The messenger handed the mandate to him as he was stepping into the pulpit. He led the congregation, all in tears, to the church gate and preached to them there.

Soon afterwards Rowlands' followers built him his own chapel in the village, where he remained their minister for another twenty-seven years. His son generously allowed him still to live at the rectory. He is buried with his wife in Llangeitho churchyard, close to the east end of the church.

John Russell
Swymington, Devon

One May afternoon, while an Oxford undergraduate, Jack Russell (1796-1883) passed a milkman with a terrier bitch in the village of Marston. Russell bought her at once. She was the hunting terrier he had been looking for. Her name was Trump and she is the ancestor of all Jack Russell terriers.

Russell was already a keen hunting man. He continued to hunt during his curacy at Iddesleigh, and when he obtained the "Perpepetual Curacy" of Swymington, he formed his own foxhunting pack. He remained at Swymington for forty-eight years, surviving the attempts of the Bishop of Exeter to end his sport. On one occasion Bishop Phillpotts dismissed Russell's curate for hunting with him, telling Russell he was sorry not to be able to dismiss him too. Finally Russell agreed to give up his pack. The bishop thanked him warmly. Russell thanked the bishop for thanking him, and said that his wife would now keep the pack.

In 1877 a fellow Master of Foxhounds wrote to Russell, "I was greatly struck by your exuberant spirits in the hunting field; much more like a schoolboy than of a man of eighty." At a tenants' ball the previous Christmas, Russell had been "among the most active dancers, joining in quadrilles, lancers, and country dances with the prettiest girls in the room". He was sorry to go to bed at three o'clock in the morning, but had to start at eight next day on a forty-mile journey to reach Lord Portsmouth's place by midday.

Russell continued to hunt at Black Torrington, where he held the living for the last four years of his life. A brass now commemorates him in the church there, but he lies buried beside his wife at Swymington.

Alexander Scott
Southminster, Essex

Alexander Scott (1768-1840) was forced to become a naval chaplain because his uncle would not pay his Cambridge debts. He served first under Lord Hood, then as chaplain of Sir Hyde Parker's flag-

ship in the West Indies, and later in the Baltic. For a time he held a living in the West Indies, but he gave it little attention.

In 1803 Nelson persuaded Scott to come as his chaplain to the Mediterranean. Here Scott also acted unofficially as Nelson's private secretary and interpreter. For Nelson he would visit Leghorn, Naples or Barcelona where, because he could obtain admission to fashionable society and because of his fluency in many languages (he spoke eight), he gained valuable information.

On Nelson's flagship, the *Victory*, Scott kept a library of 650 books. He was on deck with Nelson at the battle of Trafalgar when Nelson was shot, and he stayed with him during his dying hours. Nelson told him that he [Nelson] had "not been a great sinner". Scott rode in the procession at Nelson's funeral in January the next year, and then took up the living of Southminster.

In its parsonage Scott kept the *Victory*'s wardroom table and a number of other pieces of furniture from the ship, including a fireplace. But he lived in poverty since the Admiralty refused to add any allowance to his chaplain's half pay for his unofficial services, arguing that these had been a private arrangement with Nelson. His circumstances did not improve till 1816 when he was allowed in addition to hold the living of Catterick, and also made chaplain to the Prince Regent.

Richard Waldo Sibthorp
Ryde, Isle of Wight

Richard Sibthorp (1792-1879) was remarkable, as Gladstone put it, for having "thrice cleared the chasm which lies between the Roman and Anglican Churches". Gladstone tells less than the full story. Already at Oxford Sibthorp had run away from University College to become a Roman Catholic, but had been brought back by his elder brother and a detective. Four years later in 1815 he was ordained in the Church of England. Now a keen Evangelical, he worked in the north of England and London, then obtained the living of Ryde, Isle of Wight.

Here, however, Sibthorp was influenced by the Tractarians, introducing more and more ceremonial into his services. In 1841, four years before Newman, he became a Roman Catholic. Soon afterwards he became a Catholic priest.

Two years later Sibthorp again changed his mind and returned to the Church of England. He worked at Winchester, where he found the cathedral services depressingly dull, then in Lincolnshire, where he founded a prayer-house in memory of his mother, until 1865 when he once again became a Roman Catholic. But on his own instructions he was buried in Lincoln Cemetery with the funeral service of the Church England.

Henry Addington Simcoe
Egloskerry, Cornwall

Henry Simcoe (1800-68) came in 1826 as curate to Egloskerry near Launceston. Four years later he bought the nearby Jacobean manor house at Penheale, which he turned into a training centre for his parishioners. Here they could learn tailoring, boot-making, basket-weaving and the making of many other artefacts which could not be bought locally.

In 1846 Simcoe bought the advowson of Egloskerry and presented himself to the living. He always wore hessian boots "with a tassel exceptionally long and full suspended from them in front".

John Skelton
Diss, Norfolk

John Skelton (*c.* 1460-1529), generally considered the first poet laureate, held the living of Diss in Norfolk for twenty-five years, from 1504 till his death. Before this he had been tutor to Prince Henry, who later became Henry VIII. Skelton claimed to have taught the prince to spell.

At Diss Skelton kept a concubine by whom he had many children. When accused of fathering one of them he exhibited the boy naked in the pulpit, and asked the congregation to admit that it was "not like a pygge, nor a calfe, nor like no foule nor monstrous beast" but as fair as the best of theirs. Summoned by Richard Nix, Bishop of Norwich, to excuse himself, he brought the bishop two pheasants. When the bishop had completed his reprimand, Skelton told him that he had only one thing to say. These pheasants now had names. One was called Alpha, because it was the first pheasant he had brought him, and the other Omega, because it was the last he would bring him.

One who knew Skelton wrote that at Diss and in the diocese he was "esteemed more fit for the stage than pew or pulpit". He was especially fond of practical jokes and these were collected in a volume called *Merie Tales Newly Imprinted and made by Master Skelton, Poet Laureat*. A joke which misfired was his attack in verse on Cardinal Wolsey for his luxurious life. Tradition says that Wolsey twice imprisoned him. Not liking the experience, when Wolsey again sent to arrest him, Skelton took refuge at Westminster, where the abbot, John Islip, protected him. Here he died; he lies buried below the chancel in the Abbey.

On his death bed Skelton is said to have claimed that he was in fact married to his concubine, but had confessed to adultery (only a venial sin) rather than to marriage (at that time a capital crime for a priest).

John Skinner
Camerton, Somerset

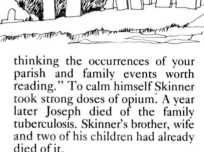

John Skinner (1772-1839) was rector of Camerton, a coal mining parish seven miles from Bristol, for thirty-nine years from 1800. When he died he left five iron chests, said to contain 146 volumes of his journals, to the British Museum, not to be opened till fifty years after his death. Ninety-eight volumes were found inside. Many described his antiquarian researches, in particular those supporting his theory that Camerton – not Colchester – was the original Roman settlement of Camulodunum.

Skinner wrote also of sickness, hardship, accidents and death in his parish. When cholera came to the village he refused to leave but buried the dead and recommended the fumigation of cottages with tobacco. He defended the poor against the rich and mean, and was horrified by such cases of neglect as that of an old man in the workhouse whose flesh was found to have been eaten away by maggots.

Despite his concern, Skinner also quarrelled continuously with his parishioners. Drunkards, Methodists and Catholics, as well as the local gentry, were his enemies. So were the village miners when they banded together.

He quarrelled with his family too, telling his son Joseph to smoke less and drink less cider, in exasperation sending his children away to Bath. In reply Joseph told him, "I suppose you will put in your journal what has taken place, and of course make it all your own way: but I don't care, I shall never read it, and whatever you may think of your great collection of MSS books, everyone, as well as myself, only laughs at your folly in thinking the occurrences of your parish and family events worth reading." To calm himself Skinner took strong doses of opium. A year later Joseph died of the family tuberculosis. Skinner's brother, wife and two of his children had already died of it.

Among Skinner's papers for the year 1839 is his *Liber Niger*, in which he recorded the fates of his enemies. His list of fifteen included:

"Charles Dando after having spent everything was killed by a fall from his horse.
"James Widcombe the Clerk and Observer was imprisoned for embezzling parish money and is now a labourer.
"Joseph Goold died in poverty and worn out by his debaucheries."

On an October morning in the same year Skinner walked from his home into a nearby beechwood and shot himself in the head with a pistol. Despite his suicide he was buried with his wife in Camerton churchyard. where his grave is still to be seen.

Charles Slingsby
Kirby-Sigston, Yorkshire

Charles Slingsby (1843-1912), rector of Kirby-Sigston from 1880 for more than twenty years, lived at Scriven, the family home of the Slingsbys; this he had inherited from his uncle, Sir Charles Slingsby, who had been drowned in the notorious Newby Ferry disaster of 1869. On that occasion eleven hunting men and their horses, in the heat of the chase, tried to cross the flooded river Ure on a small ferry boat. One of the horses plunged overboard, all rushed to that side of the ferry and it capsized. Six men were drowned.

Charles the nephew hunted regularly with the same hunt, the York and Ainsty. In 1911 he had a severe fall, breaking a rib. In 1912, now aged sixty-nine, he was thrown again, broke his neck and died instantly. A fellow hunting parson, the Rev A.S. Crowley, at once held a service over his body.

Next year two stained glass windows were dedicated to Slingsby at Moor Monkton church, where he lies buried. One shows St Hubert, patron saint of the chase, and a stag with a crucifix between its horns. The other, beside it, shows St Francis of Assisi, lover of animals and nature.

Sydney Smith
Foston-le-Clay, Yorkshire

Sydney Smith (1771-1845) held the living of Foston-le-Clay from 1806 to 1829. Few people could have been less suited to ministering to a village of three hundred Yorkshire rustics, and he resisted this fate for many years until the combined pressures of the Act of 1803, which compelled clergy to live in their parishes, and of a new Archbishop of York forced him north. Even then he settled several miles away at Heslington (where the University of York now stands), claiming that the rectory at Foston was a hovel.

From his youth Smith had been a reluctant clergyman, only taking Holy Orders when his father refused to finance him in medicine or the law. About his first living at Netheravon in Wiltshire he wrote, "Nothing can equal the immeasurable, awful dullness of this place in which I lie, dead and buried." Luckily he befriended the squire who sent him to Edinburgh as tutor to his son. Here Smith found the company of intellectuals in which he flourished, and with some of them founded the *Edinburgh Review*. Meeting secretly, they campaigned in its pages against such evils of the day as the Game Laws and conditions in the country's prisons. As a result they marked themselves for life as politically unsound in the eyes of the Establishment. "He is a very clever fellow," George III said of Smith, "but he will never be a bishop." The king was right.

In London, where Smith went next, he found his spiritual home, claiming that the "parallelogram" bounded by Oxford Street, Piccadilly, Regent Street and Hyde Park enclosed "more intelligence and human ability, to say nothing of wealth and beauty, than the world has ever collected in such a space before."

He became well known at dinner parties, made remarks which have remained funny after nearly two hundred years and coined such metaphors as "a square peg in a round hole". A friend's idea of heaven he described as "eating pâtés de foie gras to the sound of trumpets". Seeing two housewives yelling at each other from upper windows on opposite sides of St Paul's Close, he remarked that those two women would never agree since they were arguing from different premises.

Smith was a man of considerable bulk, who described himself as "of the family of Falstaff", with a broad red face and large nose. His style of humour is suggested by his comments on a large Irish lady who was to be married to a much smaller Scot:

"Marry her! Impossible! You mean a part of her: he could not marry her all himself. It would be a case, not of bigamy, but of trigamy . . . There is enough of her to furnish wives for a whole parish . . . You might people a colony with her; or give an assembly with her; or perhaps take your morning walk round her . . . provided there were frequent resting places and you were in rude health."

Resigning himself at last to residence at Foston, Smith built a commodious rectory of his own design in the middle of a field. Here, despite his urban inclinations (he described Foston as "so far out of the way that it was actually twelve miles from a lemon"), he set about becoming a contented countryman, learning to cultivate his 300-acre glebe, bake bread, brew ale, churn butter and fatten poultry. He brought a fresh mind to agriculture, as to all areas of life, installing beside the front door of his rectory a telescope to observe his labourers at work, and an enormous speaking trumpet to shout orders to them.

Finally he was rewarded by friends with a canonry at Bristol, and a less rugged parish at Combe Florey near Taunton. Soon afterwards he became a canon of St Paul's, and so could spend part of each year in London. Here he campaigned for the parliamentary Reform Bill of 1832, and made the acquaintance of such promising young men as Gladstone and Disraeli. The way in which his political views changed is summarized by his relationships with two other friends. In youth Walter Scott liked him despite his radicalism. In old age the young Dickens liked him despite his Tory opinions.

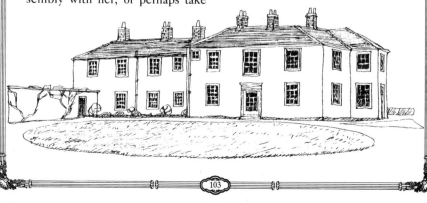

Samuel Speed
Godalming, Surrey

Samuel Speed (1631-82) was deprived of his studentship at Christ Church, Oxford for refusing to submit to the Parliamentarian visitors. Soon afterwards he fled to the West Indies, fearing that he would be accused of involvement in a plot against Cromwell. Here he became a pirate, and took part in much fighting and plundering.

After the Restoration, by which time he had taken Holy Orders, he was given the living of Godalming, but he also became chaplain to the Earl of Ossory. With this admiral he was present at the action against the Dutch on June 2nd 1665. The following couplet records Speed's behaviour on that day:

His chaplayne he plyed his wonted work
He prayed like a Christian and fought
like a Turk.

Fitzroy Henry Richard Stanhope
St Buryan, Cornwall

The Hon Fitzroy Stanhope (1787-1864), Dean of St Buryan from 1817 to 1864, had served with distinction in the Peninsular War and lost a leg at Waterloo, for which the Duke of York was unable to reward him since his pension list was exhausted. However, the duke's brother George, the Prince Regent, was able to offer Stanhope the St Buryan's deanery.

Unfortunately Stanhope could not take up this offer because he had not been ordained, and no bishop would perform the ceremony. Finally the Duke of York appealed to his friend and sycophant, the Bishop of Cork. He wrote:

"Dear Cork, kindly ordain Stanhope for me.
Yours York."

The Bishop answered:
"Dear York, Stanhope's ordained.

Yours Cork."

Stanhope employed three curates to manage the parishes of St Buryan, Sennen and St Levan respectively and never in forty-seven years visited the places himself. His total remuneration during this time is estimated to have been £60,000.

Ronald John Stephens
Stanstead Abbots, Hertfordshire

Ronald Stephens (b. 1913), vicar of Stanstead Abbots, agreed in 1970 to be the first clergyman to appear in a television commercial, on condition that he could write the forty-five-second script himself and include a "plug" for God. The advertisement was for Blue Band margarine. "I decided", he said, "to compare the need of the body for this product to the need of the soul for God. Of course I would not have agreed to the commercial if I did not believe completely in the product."

Laurence Sterne
Sutton-on-the-Forest, Yorkshire

Laurence Sterne (1713-68), author of *The Life and Opinions of Tristram Shandy, Gent.*, was born in Tipperary, the son of an unsuccessful ensign, whose regiment had just been disbanded there, but who had wealthy connections in Yorkshire.

Here in 1738 Sterne became vicar of Sutton, seven miles north of York, and for some years carried out his parish duties conscientiously. In 1741 he married Elizabeth Lumley, who claimed to be a year his junior, but according to Sterne was in fact ten years older than this. Although she brought him the additional living of Stillington, they were not compatible. The Sunday after his marriage he took for the text of his sermon "We have toiled all night and have taken nothing." About the word "wife" he wrote, "Tis a shrill penetrating sound in itself." She once "caught him with the maid, when she pulled him out of the bed on the Floor."

He was unfaithful on more occasions than this. He fell out with his uncle Jaques, Precentor and Canon of York, not only over politics but because Jaques's mistress and housekeeper, Sarah Benson, bore a daughter who had a marked resemblance to Laurence. Richard Greenwood, his servant, said that if they went to York together Sterne rarely spent a night without a girl or two, whom Richard would procure for him.

There are various opinions about Sterne's preaching, perhaps not irreconcilable. A friend wrote that whenever he preached at York Minster half the congregation left. His servant said that in his parish church he invariably reduced half the congregation to tears.

In his later years at Sutton he was a less conscientious parson and spent 1759 writing the first two volumes of *Tristram Shandy*. One night he read passages to several friends and when they did not laugh, threw the manuscript into the fire. One of them rescued it.

The book was an instant success, first in York, then in London. Sterne had anticipated this by ceasing to farm at Sutton and hiring a curate.

In 1760 he went south and was the celebrity of the year. By now he was having an affair with a singer, Catherine Fourmantel, of Huguenot origin.

Sterne's love affairs now became more frequent, or at least better documented. In 1764 he fell in love with Sarah Tuting, but she left at once for Italy. In 1765 he "flirted with certain Irish ladies" at Bath. In 1767, the year before he died, he met his best-known love, Eliza Draper, a married lady on leave from India. When she left to rejoin her husband he wrote *Letters from Yorick to Eliza* for her, his final book.

Before he had ceased to write the latter he was sending passionate notes to an unknown Hannah. He died suddenly the following March. His brother-in-law, the Rev John Botham, at once hurried from his parish in Surrey and burned "a large parcel of Letters of Love and Gallantry from Ladies of the first Rank and Quality".

Sterne was buried in St George's, Hanover Square, Burial Ground, Paddington, where, according to Hall-Stevenson, his fellow Yorkshire parson, his body was stolen for anatomical experiments at Oxford.

When the site of his grave was excavated in 1968 (before flats were built there by the Utopian Housing Society) a skull was found with its top sawn off, and other bones which for size might have been Sterne's. Conceivably the thieves, discovering that they had taken such a famous body, returned and reburied it.

Sterne's house at Coxwold is preserved as a memorial to him.

Edward Stokes
Blaby, Leicestershire

Though totally blind from the age of nine, Edward Stokes (1706-98) obtained two good Leicestershire livings, holding the second at Blaby for fifty years from 1748 till he died at the age of ninety-two. He had been blinded in an accident. He and his brothers were playing with a pistol which they did not know was loaded. He had previously snapped it close to the breast of a young lady. The last sight he remembered before telling his brother to fire it at him was what he believed to be the bottom of the pistol's empty barrel, but was in fact the paper wadding of the charge. His face was filled with shot which continued to come out all his life, one piece as late as two years before he died. His brother is said to have died young of distress.

Stokes took church services with only the help of one person to read the lessons and, as well as preaching, would sometimes recite the collects or psalms. He was always cheerful and would walk about his own pre-

mises with no guide, so that strangers often did not realize he was blind. He spent most of his handsome fortune on helping the poor of the village.

He used to "hunt briskly", but was always accompanied by a person who "when a leap was to be taken, rang a bell".

William Stukeley
Stamford, Lincolnshire

William Stukeley (1687-1765), famed for his research on Stonehenge and Avebury, showed first an interest in animal biology.

For seven years Stukeley was a doctor at Boston, Lincolnshire, then moved to London, where he continued to practise. When an elephant died there he helped his friend Sir Hans Sloane dissect it in his Chelsea

garden and published his *Essay towards the Anatomy of the Elephant*, in which he suggests that the elephant's illness was "heightened by the great quantity of ale the spectators continually gave it".

Already he had become a well-known antiquary. He made many trips about the country and became especially interested in stone circles

which he attributed to the Druids. When he left London in 1726 to live at Grantham he built in his garden there a wooded Druids' temple. At this time he married; presently he buried the embryo of his wife's second miscarriage below his Druid high altar "with ceremonies proper to the occasion".

Stukeley was ordained next year (1727), in order to find himself a better livelihood and more peace than doctoring allowed, and soon afterwards obtained the living of All Saints, Stamford. He managed to reconcile Christianity and Druidism by the ingenious suggestion that the Druids were originally a colony of Phoenicians who had come to England in Abraham's time, who were "of *Abraham's* religion intirely". By their own reasoning they had developed a religion which only

differed from Christianity in that they still expected a Messiah.

Thus his books, *Stonehenge* and *Abury*, which he completed over the next thirteen years, were meant to "combat the deists from an unexpected quarter". The excellent early field work he had done was, in the words of Stuart Piggott, his biographer, "entangled with the most curious mixture of Biblical and classical allusions and flights of the wildest etymological fancies".

In 1747, tiring of country life, he took the London living of St George's, Bloomsbury, where at the age of seventy-six, preaching in spectacles for the first time in his life, he used the text, "Now we see through a glass darkly." He is buried without monument in the churchyard of East Ham.

George Henry Sumner
Old Alresford, Hampshire

George Sumner (1824-1909) held the living of Old Alresford for thirty-four years from 1851. He was the son of the Bishop of Winchester, and himself later became Bishop of Guildford. He is remembered as the husband of Mary Sumner, who founded the Mothers' Union, an organization to include "lady mothers" as well as "cottage mothers".

As rector of Old Alresford, Sumner had a comfortable income of £580 a year (though much less than his predecessor, Francis North, who held the parish with three other livings). It took one servant the whole morning to trim and fill the forty lamps Sumner's household required, and Mary Sumner is said never in her life to have put on her own stockings. She survived her husband and wrote a panegyric memoir of him in which she describes her own participation in Old Alresford village concerts: "Mrs Sumner was the heart and soul of these; and being a very accomplished and trained singer delighted her audiences with arias from the Italian operas, Handel's oratorios and simple English ballads."

William Sweetaple
Fledborough, Nottinghamshire

William Sweetaple (1688-1755), rector of Fledborough for forty-three years from 1712, was made a surrogate for issuing marriage licences in 1729 and thereafter carried out 490 marriages, all but fifteen of them between parties living outside his village. He thus performed for English eloping couples a service they later went across the Scottish border to Gretna and like places to obtain. Beside the road near his village he erected a sign reading "To Fledborough and No Further". He died in 1755, two years after the Marriage Act made practices of this sort illegal.

Thomas Teasdale
Luckington, Wiltshire

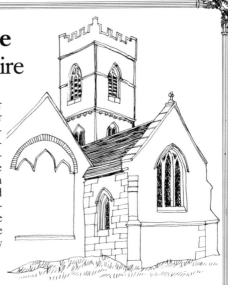

Thomas Teasdale (1801-64), poor curate of Luckington near Alderton in the mid-nineteenth century, supported a family of five children on his £80 stipend while compiling a Greek lexicon. When he had been working at this for ten years, Liddell and Scott published their lexicon, so rendering Teasdale's labour useless. Presently he "removed to Hullavington where he gradually in extreme penury wasted away."

John Tench
Great Rollright, Oxfordshire

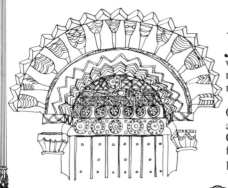

John Tench (1766-1848), rector of Great Rollright from 1811 to 1848, was appointed to this living by Brasenose College, Oxford, where he had not been popular.

On returning to Oxford after an absence Tench was described by Cox in his reminiscences as "an odd fish . . . wearing a vulgar-looking powdered one-curled wig, speaking with a strong Lancashire dialect, and reading with a voice of thunder: indeed his enunciation of the oaths and exhortations on Degree-days was an awful infliction on the drums of one's ear." The Principal of the college recorded that he always wore "nasty fustian breeches and filthy worsted stockings".

Perhaps as a consequence of Tench's loudness and aggressiveness, two Nonconformist chapels were built in the village during his time there. He died at the age of eighty-two in Chipping Norton, where he had lived for the last eighteen months, but was brought back to Great Rollright for burial.

George Tennyson
Somersby & Bag Enderby, Lincolnshire

George Tennyson (1778-1831), was vicar of the two tiny villages of Somersby and Bag Enderby near Horncastle in north Lincolnshire, which together had only about two hundred inhabitants. He was embittered for life by his father's preference for his younger brother, Charles Tennyson D'Eyncourt, to whom he ultimately left his fortune. George Tennyson would fall into deep depressions and take comfort in bouts of heavy drinking. But he was a tall, good-looking man with an interest in poetry and a library unusually large for a parson of the time in a remote country living.

He had twelve children, whom he treated sternly, in contrast to his wife who spoiled them.

Belatedly, George's father obtained for him the living at Grimsby nearby, which enabled him to employ a curate and buy fine claret from London, but he still sent his children to the village school, then to Louth Grammar School. At home he taught them the classics himself, so enabling Frederick, Charles and Alfred his fourth son to go to Trinity College, Cambridge.

Less than a month after Alfred's return from Cambridge, George died of a stroke, leaning back in his chair in his library. Because of the family's subsequent poverty both Frederick and Charles took Holy Orders, though Alfred refused.

Robert Stuart Thomas
Eglwys Fach, Pembrokeshire

The poet R.S. Thomas was born in 1913 in Cardiff and brought up partly in Liverpool. He was rector of Manafon in Montgomeryshire for twelve years from 1942 and here published his first three volumes of poems. He went next to be vicar of Eglwys Fach in north Pembrokeshire where he stayed till 1967, publishing five more volumes. Since then he has been vicar of Eglwys Hywyn Sant at Aberdaron at the end of the Llŷn Peninsula, where he has been even more prolific. He has won many prizes, including the 1964 Queen's Gold Medal for Poetry.

In his fifties Thomas said of his own poetry, "I play on a small pipe, a little aside from the main road." But lately he has written in a more general way of Wales.

Thomas has remained a private person and little is known, perhaps because there is little to know, about his parish life. He will probably be thought the most important Welsh poet of the century, Dylan Thomas not excluded.

John Thomlinson
Glenfield, Leicestershire

John Thomlinson (1692-1761) was at first curate to his uncle John in the Northumberland parish of Rothbury, where he recorded in his diary the gossip of the day, for example:

"1718 Sept 14th. The bishop of Durham's lady once paying a visit to the new mayor – while her coach stood at the door, some putt a ball of hair full of lice into the seat – they run up her back and to her neck, forced to strip – the bishop would give £40 to know the person . . ."

He also reported on his two chief interests: finding a wife and getting a living of his own. Uncle John pressed Dolly Collingwood on him, but he found her like a Flanders mare, and the dinner provided by her father very mean, though admittedly there was a bottle of wine.

So he courted Elizabeth Ord and Judith Wheler, becoming so uncertain which he wanted that on February 14th 1718 he put both their names into a hat. He does not say whose came out first. He seems to have enjoyed his philandering reputation, and wrote that friends "would call [me] Jack among th' women, for I was always among 'em". But sometimes there was a note of desperation in his planning:

"1718 April 8th. Told namesake I had tryed one woman and did not like her, I was to try another shortly, for some overtures had been made, etc., and if I found her answer the description etc., I intended to attack her very briskly and reduce her by storm."

Meanwhile another uncle, Robert, "had rather I had Mr Douglas' daughter than Dolly Collingwood but he has one in view with £3,000 whose father is the most likely man to gett me a living of any man he knows."

Three years later he was still unmarried and involved with Miss Tod, but gave her up because she gossiped, in favour of Nancy Repington. "Jan 10th 1722. N. Lay in my bosom the night before I came . . ."

On the following days he sent letters to his father asking for a marriage settlement which would match Nancy's. But by mid March he was considering the Bishop of Durham's daughter, and by the end of March the Bishop of London's.

Earlier he had told himself about his future wife that it was "a very material point to have one could gett me a living." This is the advice he ultimately took. By June 1722 he was married to Catherine Winstanley, whose father presented him to the rectory of Glenfield three miles from Leicester, where he stayed for the rest of his life.

Augustus Montague Toplady
Broadhembury, Devon

Augustus Toplady (1740-78) was at first Evangelically inclined, but from the age of eighteen devoted his life to little else except violent opposition to John Wesley. In 1766 he became vicar of Hapford, then two years later moved to Broadhembury which he held for the rest of his life. On hearing that Hapford vicarage had burned down soon after he handed it over to a friend, he wrote in his diary, "What a providential mercy was it that I resigned the living before this misfortune happened!"

Toplady wrote scurrilous verses against Wesley in the *Gospel Magazine.* He wrote the well-known hymn *Rock*

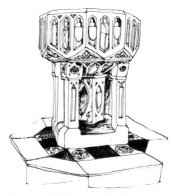

of ages, cleft for me while in a gorge of the Mendips. But a large part of his life was spent preaching in London. Here his conflict with Wesley involved "every possible expression of virulent contempt . . . on both sides."

When Toplady, on his death bed, heard of a report that he had changed his view he had himself carried to the pulpit of Orange Street Chapel where he denied it, and denied too that he had asked to see Wesley. "I most sincerely hope", he said, "my last hours will be much better employed than in conversation with such a man."

Thomas Traherne
Credenhill, Herefordshire

For two hundred years after his death Thomas Traherne (1636-74) was forgotten, until in 1896 two manuscript collections of his poems were found in a street bookstall by William Brooke. Brooke consulted Dr Grosart and both concluded that they were the work of Henry Vaughan – indeed Grosart planned an elaborate edition of Vaughan's poetry in which they were to be included. Only the detective work of Bertram Dobell discovered their real author; Dobell bought them and published them in 1903. Together with Traherne's prose writings (*Centuries of Meditation* and *Christian Ethicks*), his mystical poems make him a key figure in an understanding of the religious ideas of his time.

Traherne was born in Hereford, the son of a shoemaker, but the date of his birth is guesswork, based on the years he is known to have been at Brasenose College, Oxford. From Oxford he went to the parish of Credenhill in Herefordshire. Ten years later he became chaplain to Sir Orlando Bridgman and moved to Teddington, where he died at the early age of about thirty-eight.

Among the little known of Traherne's life are two supernatural experiences recorded by John Aubrey. In one Traherne saw an apprentice "sitting in a chair in his red waistcoat, and head band about his head, and strap upon his knee; which apprentice was really in bed asleep with another fellow apprentice." In the other, a basket of fruit "came sailing in the air along the valence of his bed". More revealingly, the introduction to Traherne's posthumous *Serious and Pathetical Contemplations* says that he was a man so full of divine thoughts that "those who would converse with him were forced to endure some discourse upon these subjects, whether they had any sense of Religion or not. And therefore to such he might be sometimes thought troublesome."

He died so poor that in his own opinion it was only worth his making a verbal will. By this he left his best Hatt to his brother Phillipp, charging his sister-in-law Susan to keep it for him, and his old Hatt "to Phillipp Landman or to whome you please."

Nicholas Udall
Braintree, Essex

The reputation of Nicholas Udall (1505-56) rests on his only surviving play, *Ralf Roister Doister*, the earliest known English comedy, a homely work on the Latin model, in rhyming doggerel. A first version of this was written for the boys of Eton where Udall was headmaster for eight years.

Here Thomas Tusser records that he received fifty-three stripes (with the cane) from Udall for "fault but small or none at all". Udall's headmastership ended in scandal when he was charged with complicity in a theft of silver images and plate from the college, and of unnatural vices. Brought before the Privy Council, he confessed to the second charge and was sent to Marshalsea prison.

But the sentence was brief and on release he became vicar of Braintree in Essex, holding the living from 1537 to 1544.

All his life Udall survived with skill the various political changes of the times, flirting with Lutheranism at Oxford, writing verses for the pageant to welcome Anne Boleyn to London after her marriage to Henry VIII, patronized in turn by Henry's later wife Catherine Parr, next by the Protestant Edward VI, and then by Queen Mary, for whom he tried to extract a recantation from an imprisoned Protestant martyr, Thomas Mountain. Finally he became headmaster of a second great school, Westminster; he lies buried in Westminster Abbey.

Henry Venn
Yelling, Huntingdonshire

Henry Venn (1725-97) was one of a family of parish priests. His direct paternal ancestors had held livings, chiefly in Devon, for four generations, and his son and grandson were also parsons.

As a young man at Jesus College, Cambridge, he was a keen cricketer. In 1747, after playing for Surrey against All England in front of "a very considerable body of spectators" he flung down his bat, declaring "I am to be ordained on Sunday; and I will never have it said of me, 'Well struck, Parson.'" He kept his promise.

He was first a curate at West Horsley, then at Clapham. At this time he also held two lectureships in London and would regularly preach six ser-mons a week. He then moved to Huddersfield where he became a leading Evangelical. Twelve years later when he left this "huge, dark, ignorant, immoral, irreligious manu-facturing town" he had "shaken [it] to the centre by the lever of the gospel." So hard had he worked that he was coughing and spitting blood and showing other signs of advanced consumption. He retired to Yelling, in Huntingdonshire.

Here he found the hundred parish-ioners of this small village "sitting in darkness, ignorant of the first principles of the gospel". His health, however, recovered and he held the living for twenty-six years. He died at Clapham, where his son had be-come rector and is buried in the old churchyard there.

Robert Walker
Seathwaite, Cumberland

Robert Walker (1709-1802), the Cumberland curate who became known in his lifetime as "Wonderful Walker", was born the youngest of twelve, in the little village of Seathwaite in Borrowdale. He became a curate there at the age of twenty-five and held the same position till his death at the age of ninety-three. His initial annual stipend was £5. Even with tithes and other extras his income amounted only to £20 annually. Nevertheless, he brought up a family of eight children, and when in 1756 he was offered the nearby curacy of Ulpha to add to his own, he refused it in case he should seem greedy. He augmented his income by spinning, at which craft he was "a great proficient". He would sit spinning while his parish children repeated their lessons to him.

In Book *vii* of *The Excursion* Wordsworth writes of Walker:

> *. . . and him the WONDERFUL*
> *Our simple shepherds, speaking from*
> *the heart*
> *Deservedly have styled . . .*

Despite his poverty Walker died leaving £2,000. He was buried in Seathwaite churchyard; a brass plate in the church commemorates him.

Samuel Walker
Truro, Cornwall

Though the Evangelical preacher Samuel Walker (1714-61) held the livings of the Cornish parishes of Lanlivery and Talland, he is remembered for his time at the county town of Truro, where he was curate in charge from 1746 for fourteen years. He took the position because he was addicted to the dancing and card playing to be found in this fashionable place, but experienced a conversion when the headmaster of Truro Grammar School sent him some unpaid duty on wine to be passed on to the collector of taxes.

His conversion was total, and he became known for his hostility to pleasure of all kinds. Certain discontented parishioners asked the non-resident rector of Truro to dismiss him, but though the rector made two attempts he was too embarrassed to say the necessary words.

The citizens of Truro were, for the most part, equally impressed by Walker. When he preached at St Mary's it was said that you could have fired a cannon down any street in the town and hit no one. Though Walker was friendly with Wesley and admired by him he never became a Methodist. Hard work presently brought on tuberculosis and he died at Blackheath at the early age of forty-six.

John Ward
Great Bedwyn & East Grafton, Wiltshire

John Ward (1795-1861), vicar of Great Bedwyn and East Grafton from 1826 to 1850, infected by the church-building enthusiasm of the times, planned a fine new church for East Grafton. It was to be in Norman style with a stone barrel roof, "interior and exterior one mass of masonry". Despite warnings he persisted, adding for safety internal flying buttresses in the side aisles. In 1843 when Sidney Herbert wanted to see the new church a date was arranged for April, though this was earlier than Ward or his architect would have liked. Herbert brought with him a relation, Mr Montgomery, "an amiable and excellent man, of great taste, and fond of church architecture".

Together they watched while the wooden supporting cradle was lowered. The barrel roof seemed to hold, then entirely collapsed; a massive stone rebounded off the scaffolding and struck Montgomery, killing him instantly.

The wetness of the mortar was believed to be the cause of the collapse, rather than faulty design. Nevertheless Ward abandoned his stone roof for a wooden one. "Indeed", said Mozley, "he would never have got a congregation to sit under it."

Francis J. Waring
Heybridge, Essex

Francis Waring (d. 1833), vicar of Heybridge from 1798, was renowned for the speed with which he conducted church services, which he timed with a small clock. He needed to hurry in order to ride away and take services at his other two churches.

Waring habitually wore eccentric dress, would often change his costume three times a day, and was reprimanded by his bishop for wearing purple on a formal occasion.

For variety on Wednesdays he would dress as a Quaker.

He believed that houses should be built around a central passage, but had his own built so narrow that, being a large man, he alone could pass. He made his children feed from a trough, and slept with his wife in a large wicker rocking cradle. When insulted at a public dinner by the mayor of a neighbouring village, a Mr Bugg who looked like a bulldog, Waring replied by barking.

Samuel Wesley
Epworth, Lincolnshire

The life of Samuel Wesley (1662-1735), father of the Methodist brothers John and Charles, was much affected by misfortune, some of his own making.

At Oxford Wesley was first a poet, and published *Maggots: or, Poems on Several Subjects, never before handled.* After taking Holy Orders he became chaplain of a man-of-war, then rector of South Ormsby, where he lived in a "mean cot". He was forced to

resign this living because he refused to allow the mistress of the Marquis of Normanby, who had a house in the parish, to visit his rectory.

When he became rector of Epworth in 1697 he was already £150 in debt and three years later his debts had doubled. By then his barn had fallen down. In 1702 fire partially destroyed his rectory.

By this time there had been

published, without his consent, a private letter he had written to a friend disclosing inside information about the practices in Nonconformist academies. This brought him into disfavour with dissenters.

In 1709 Wesley's rebuilt rectory was again destroyed by fire. His parishioners, who disliked his High Church opinions and had already stabbed his cows, now set the rectory alight by throwing burning torches on to its thatch. With it went his early work for his major study of the *Book of Job*. Thereafter he was so incapacitated by gout and palsy that he employed an assistant to write it.

The volume, dedicated to Queen Caroline, was not finally published until after his death. When Wesley's son gave the queen a copy she remarked, "It is very prettily bound."

For two months during the winter of 1716-17 mysterious noises disturbed the again rebuilt rectory at Epworth. All over the house were heard knockings, groans and rattlings as of metal pans, windows and door latches. A period free from dramatic incident followed till 1731, when Wesley was thrown from a wagon and severely injured. He died four years later and is buried in Epworth churchyard.

George White
Colne, Lancashire

In 1748 George White, curate of Colne, infuriated by the preaching of William Grimshaw in his parish and by Methodism in general, issued this proclamation: "Notice is hereby given that if any man be mindful to enlist in his Majesty's Service under the command of the Revd. George White, Commander-in-Chief . . . let him repair to the drum-head at the Cross, where each man shall receive a pint of ale in advance . . ." The private army he thus raised engaged the supporters of Grimshaw and John Wesley at Roughlee and "made them run for their lives, amidst showers of dirt and stones, without any regard to age or sex. Some of them they trampled in the mire and dragged by the hair . . . many they beat with their clubs without mercy."

White regularly carried with him a pistol but is not said to have used it on this occasion. He died of drink.

Gilbert White
Selborne, Hampshire

Gilbert White (1720-93) was born in the little village of Selborne, near Alton. At the age of seven, when his father died, his family took up residence in a house across the road, now called The Wakes. Here, after a further sixty-six years, he died at the age of seventy-three. He was four times curate at Selborne, including for the last nine years of his life. His longest curacy was at Farringdon, two miles away, which he held for twenty-two years, but his light duties there enabled him still to live at The Wakes. Though he travelled widely in the south of England, he suffered from coach sickness, and never went further north than Derbyshire. He described the South Downs as a "vast range of mountains".

White never married. The only woman he may have been emotionally involved with was Hester Muslo. He called her "Hecky"; she called him "Whitey-bus". The affair did not prosper.

The letters which form his classic work, *The Natural History of Selborne*, were addressed to the eminent zoologist, Thomas Pennant, and to the explorer and naturalist, Daines Barrington. They span the years 1767-87, and were for the most part genuine letters, though a few may have been added to complete White's picture of Selborne.

White's careful and precise observations are in the scientific tradition of today, but some of his beliefs were quaint. The theory of the migration of birds was already known but to the end of his life he remained unconvinced that all flew away, and would climb in winter to Selborne hangar and poke about in the bushes for hibernating swallows.

Much that he describes can still be seen at Selborne, including the zig-zag path to the hangar with the hermitage which he built there for picnics, and the 1,000-year-old yew tree, its trunk twenty-three feet in circumference in White's time, eight inches larger when Cobbett measured it in August 1823.

William Carus Wilson
Casterton, Yorkshire

Carus Wilson (1791-1859), a pious and industrious churchman, achieved notoriety when he was easily identified as Mr Brocklehurst, "the black-marble clergyman" in Charlotte Brontë's *Jane Eyre*, the founder of a school for the daughters of the clergy. Mrs Gaskell, in her life of Charlotte Brontë, accuses Wilson of gross mismanagement of the school at Cowan Bridge, to which four of the Brontë sisters went briefly.

It was the two miles to Wilson's church at Turnstall that the Brontë children were forced to walk on Sundays in all weathers, a bitterly cold walk in winter "especially to children whose thin blood flowed languidly in consequence of their half-starved condition". They were half-starved because the school's food was so repulsively cooked and served that they often could not bear to eat it. Mrs Gaskell is careful never to accuse Wilson of malicious intentions, but of incompetence in choosing staff, and of "perpetual injudicious interference with the details" of the running of the school.

All his life Wilson was a founder of schools; despite his embarassment at Cowan Bridge he went on founding them. In 1841 he had four concentrated at Casterton: the clergymen's daughters school, a servants' school, a preparatory school and a village school. By this time he had resigned the living of Turnstall, but held Whittington and Casterton. He had also founded two religious newspapers.

James Woodforde
Weston Longueville, Norfolk

James Woodforde (1740-1803), rector of Weston Longueville, was forgotten till 1924 when John Beresford published his diaries and made him the best known of all eighteenth-century English parsons. His utterly undistinguished life, as described in the five volumes which form Beresford's selection (there was enough material to make twelve), gives the fullest picture we have of a country parson of his period.

Woodforde kept his diary for forty-three years, from his time at New College, Oxford, to his death in 1803. In it he describes the vast dinners he ate (he was a light breakfaster), the games he played for money with neighbours (cards in winter, bowls in summer), his relations with his niece Nancy (he was never married), his visits to the West Country where he at first held curacies, and how he farmed his glebe. His religious duties and gifts to the poor are regularly mentioned, but without comment.

Typically, for December 31st 1780 he writes: "This being the last day of the year we sat up till after 12 o'clock, then drank a Happy New Year to all our Friends and went to bed. We were very merry indeed after supper till 12. Nancy and Betsie Davie locked me into the great Parlour, and both fell on me and pulled my Wigg almost to Pieces. – I paid them for it however."

Andrew John Young
Stonegate, Sussex

Andrew Young (1885-1971), poet, was born in Elgin and educated in Edinburgh, where he at one time played truant on principle, having decided that school, unlike prison, was an institution to which inmates were committed without trial. Returning, he had a successful academic career and became a Presbyterian minister. In 1939 after ministering at Hove in Sussex for nineteen years, he joined the Church of England. For a short time he was curate at Plaistow, then in 1941 obtained the living of Stonegate where he remained for eighteen years.

He was a man of great impracticality. He did not understand electricity and though he had a car for several years he never knew its make. He used an antique typewriter, in which the ribbon was struck by the keys from below. When speaking on the telephone he would begin without preamble, for example, "My central heating's broken", or "Where shall I go for a new suit?" He would write at great length then continually refine his work until he had reduced it to a few lines or paragraphs.

His friendships were improbably wide, and at his services more than one of such well known people as Christopher Hassall or John Arlott would read the lessons. On New Year's Eve he was known to sit up all night drinking whisky with John Arlott. But he had no small talk and would sit in silence for an hour with a sick parishioner before rising abruptly and saying he must go.

He was a keen naturalist and considerable expert on wild flowers; he claimed to have given up bird watching because his parishioners, seeing him with binoculars, would believe he was off to the races. He was addicted to televised wrestling and would sit watching it all afternoon, but if discovered would explain "Janet loves it", though his wife was not even in the room.

When he retired to the small village of Yapton he bought the first house he was shown, failing to discover that there was not a bus service, so he had no way of reaching Chichester. He had already published his *Collected Poems* in 1936 and 1950. At Yapton he published several further books including *The Poet and the Landscape* and *The new and Poly-Olbion*. He died at the age of eighty-six and was cremated.

Bibliography

ADDISON, WILLIAM, *The English Country Parson*, Dent, 1947
ANDERSON, Verily, *The Last of the Eccentrics*, Hodder & Stoughton, 1972
AUBREY, John, *Brief Lives*, edited by Oliver Lawson Dick, Secker & Warburg, 1949

BARING-GOULD, Sabine, *The Church Revival*, Methuen, 1914
BARING-GOULD, Sabine, *The Vicar of Morwenstow*, Methuen, 1899
BARROW, Andrew, *The Flesh is Weak*, Hamish Hamilton, 1980
BATTISCOMBE, Georgina, *John Keble*, Constable, 1963
BENTLEY, James, *Ritualism and Politics in Victorian Britain*, 1978
BERESFORD, J., See WOODFORD, James
BLACKBURNE, Neville, *The Restless Ocean*, Terence Dalton, 1972
BLOMEFIELD, Francis, *Essay Towards a Topographical History of Norfolk*, William Miller, 1750
BLYTHE, Ronald, *The Age of Illusion*, Hamish Hamilton, 1963
BRENDON, Piers, *Hawker of Morwenstow*, Cape, 1975
BRONTË, Charlotte, *Jane Eyre*, Smith Elder, 1847
BROWN, C. K. Francis, *A History of the English Clergy*, Faith Press, 1953
BUTLER, Samuel, *The Way of All Flesh*, Grant Richards, 1903
BYLES, C. E., *The Life and Letters of R. S. Hawker*, John Lang, 1905

CAULFIELD, Catherine, *The Emperor of the United States of America*, Routledge & Kegan Paul, 1981
CHAMBERS, R., (editor), *The Book of Days*, W. & R. Chambers, 1863
CHAPMAN, Ronald, *Father Faber*, Burns & Oates, 1961
CHITTY, Susan, *The Beast and the Monk*, Hodder & Stoughton, 1974
CLERGY LISTS, John Murray
COLE, William, *Blencheley Diary of William Cole*, edited by F. G. Stokes, Constable, 1931
COLLOMS, Brenda, *Victorian Country Parsons*, Constable, 1977
COOMBS, Joyce, *George and Mary Sumner*, Sumner Press, 1965
CROCKFORD'S CLERICAL DIRECTORIES, Oxford University Press

DANIELS, W. B., *Rural Sports*, Longman, Hurst, Rees & Orme, 1801
DAVIES, E. W. L., *Memoir of the Rev. John Russell*, Richard Bentley, 1878
DAVIES, G. C. B., *The Early Cornish Evangelicals 1735-60*, S.P.C.K., 1951
DICTIONARY OF NATIONAL BIOGRAPHY, Smith Elder
DU MAURIER, Daphne, *Vanishing Cornwall*, Gollancz, 1967

EDE, John F., *History of Wednesbury*, Wednesbury Corporation, 1962
ELLIOTT-BINNS, L. E., *The Early Evangelicals*, Lutterworth Press, 1953
ESCOTT, Thomas Hay Sweet, *Society in the Country House*, T. Fisher Unwin, 1907
EWBANK, Jane M., *The Life and Works of William Carus Wilson*, Titus Wilson, 1959

FABER, Geoffrey, *Oxford Apostles*, Faber, 1933
FAIRFAX-LUCY, Alice, *Charlecote and the Lucys*, Oxford University Press, 1958
FITZSIMONS, John, (editor), *Manning, Anglican and Catholic*, Burns Oates, 1951
FOSTER, Joseph, *Alumni Oxonienses*, James Parker, 1891
FOX, Adam, *English Hymns and Hymn Writers*, Collins, 1947
FULLER, Thomas, *History of the Worthies of England*, British Museum Catalogue, 1662

GASKELL, Mrs, *The Life of Charlotte Brontë*, Smith Elder, 1857
GREEN, V. H. H., *Oxford Common Room*, Edward Arnold, 1957

HAMMOND, Peter C., *The Parson and the Victorian Parish*, Hodder & Stoughton, 1977
HART, A. Tindal, *The Country Parson in Elizabethan and Stuart Times*, Phoenix House, 1958
HART, A. Tindal, *The Country Priest in English History*, Phoenix House, 1959
HART, A. Tindal, *The Curate's Lot*, John Baker, 1970
HART, A. Tindal, *The Eighteenth Century Country Parson*, Wilding & Sons, 1955
HENDERSON, Charles, *Essays in Cornish History*, Clarendon, 1935
HENDERSON, Philip, *Samuel Butler*, Cohen & West, 1967
HINDE, Thomas, *Sir Henry and Sons*, Macmillan, 1980
HOLE, S. R., *Memoirs of Dean Hole*, Arnold, 1893
HOUSTON, Mrs M. C., *A Woman's Memories of World-known Men*, F. V. White, 1883
HUMPHREYS, A. L., *Eccentric Characters of Berkshire*, Berks, Bucks & Oxon Archeological Journal, 1926

JEFFREY, R. W., *The Manors and Advowsons of Great Rollright*, Oxfordshire Record Society, 1927
JONES, William, *The Diary of the Rev. William Jones*, edited by C. F. Christie, Brentano's, 1929

KETTON-CREMER, R. W., *Country Neighbourhood*, Faber, 1951
KETTON-CREMER, R. W., *Norfolk Assembly*, Faber, 1957
KILVERT, Francis, *Diary of the Rev. Francis Kilvert*, edited by W. Plomer, Cape, 1938-40

LOCK, John and Dixon, Canon W. T. *Brontë, A Man of Sorrow*, Nelson, 1965

MABEY, Richard, *Introduction to the Natural History of Selborne*, Penguin, 1977
MARTIN, R. B., *Enter Rumour*, Faber, 1962
MARTIN, W. Keble, *Over the Hills*, Michael Joseph, 1968
MASSINGHAM, Betty, *Turn on the Fountains*, Gollancz, 1974
MATTHEWS, A. G., *Walker Revised*, Oxford University Press, 1948
McCLATCHEY, Diana, *Oxfordshire Clergy 1777-1869*, Oxford University Press, 1960
MENZIES, Stuart, *Sportsmen Parsons in Peace and War*, Hutchinson, 1919
MERCHANT, W. Moelwyn, *R. S. Thomas*, 1979
MOZLEY, Thomas, *Reminiscences*, Longman Green, 1882

OLLARD, S. L., (editor), *Dictionary of English Church History*, Mowbray, 1912

PARISH, William, *Dictionary of the Sussex Language*, Lewes, 1875
PEARSON, Hesketh, *The Smith of Smiths*, Hamish Hamilton, 1934
PIGGOTT, Stuart, *William Stukeley*, 1950
PLOMER, William, *'Francis Kilvert', Essays by Divers Hands*, Royal Literary Society, 1975
PONSONBY, Arthur, *English Diaries*, Methuen, 1923
PUTTERILL, Jack, *Thaxted Quest for Social Justice*

REDDING, Cyrus, *Memoirs of Remarkable Misers*, Charles H. Skeet, 1863
ROGERS, Benjamin, *Diary of Benjamin Rogers*, edited by C. D. Linnell, Bedfordshire Historical Records
     Society, 1949
ROUS, John, *Diary of John Rous*, edited by M. A. E. Green, Camden Society, 1856

SKINNER, John, *Journal of a Somerset Rector, 1803-34*, Kingsmead, 1971
STRACHEY, Lytton, *Eminent Victorians*, Chatto, 1918
SYKES, N., *Church and State in England in the Eighteenth Century*, Adam & Charles Black, 1934

THOMLINSON, John, *Diary of John Thomlinson*, 1834
THOMPSON, Flora, *Lark Rise to Candleford*, Oxford University Press, 1939-43
THOMSON, David, *Wild Excursions*, Weidenfeld, 1972
TIMBS, John, *English Eccentrics and Eccentricities*, Richard Bentley, 1866
TRAHERNE, Thomas, *Poetical Works of Thomas Traherne*, edited by Gladys I. Wade, P. T. & A. E. Dobell, 1932
TURNER, Thomas, *Diary of Thomas Turner of East Hoathly*, Bodley Head, 1925
TYREMAN, Rev. L., *The Life of John Wesley*, Hodder, 1871

VENN, John, and Venn, J. A., *Alumni Cantabrigienses*, Cambridge University Press, 1922

WALKER, John, *The Sufferings of the Clergy during the Great Rebellion*, London, 1714
WARNE, Arthur, *Church and Society in Eighteenth Century Devon*, David & Charles, 1969
WHITE, Gilbert, *The Natural History of Selborne 1788-89*, London
WOODFORD, James, *Diary of a Country Parson*, edited by J. Beresford, Oxford University Press, 1924-31
WOOLF, Virginia, *Common Reader Second Series*, Hogarth Press, 1932

Acknowledgements

Extracts from the following books have been quoted in *A Field Guide to the English Country Parson*:

Page 52 (Charles Sawkins Harrison): *Lark Rise to Candleford*, Flora Thompson, Oxford University Press, 1939

Page 67 (Charles Kingsley Senior): *The Beast and the Monk*, Susan Chitty, Hodder & Stoughton, 1974; with
     the permission of Curtis Brown.

Page 101 (John Skinner): *Journal of a Somerset Rector, 1803-34*, Kingsmead, 1971